Read carefully this personal and powerful story by Jeannie Smith as she portrays God's hand of provision as she and her husband were obedient in the small and big things of life.

I have watched this obedience over the years and I've seen God's promises come true.

It is a quick read but one filled with encouragement.

Dr. Frank Page, President/CEO
Southern Baptist Executive Committee

If you Love Me Obey Me

The Secret to Purpose and Freedom

By: Jeannie Scott Smith

If you Love Me Obey Me
Copyright © 2017
Jeannie Scott Smith.

All rights reserved. No part of this publication may be reproduced, stored in a retrieval system, or transmitted in any way by any means—electronic, mechanical, photocopy, recording, or otherwise—without the prior permission of the copyright holder, except as provided by USA copyright law.

Unless otherwise noted, all Scriptures are taken from the Bible text used in this edition of the Life Application Study Bible is the
Holy Bible, King James Version.

Cover Design: 4foursite

Comments:
jeanniescottsmith.com

ISBN: 978-1-941069-78-3

Prose Press
Pawleys Island, SC
prosencons@live.com

Dedication:

This piece of work is an offering to my greatest friend, teacher, and love, Jesus.

Contents

The Invitation 1

1. Shattered into Beautiful: Our Heart 15

2. The Scary Unknown: Our Will 35

3. Time for Battle: Our Mind 65

4. Receiving the Miracle: Our Body 65

5. The Gift: Our Finances 85

6. First Love: Our Future 101

Bibliography 122

Acknowledgements:

I would like to thank my Father in Heaven who entrusted this project to me. Thank you for all the blessings and gifts you have given me for simply obeying.

To my husband, Carter, thank you for the unconditional love you give me, for humbly serving me, and for the endless hours you have unselfishly given me to finish this work.

To my friend, Marsha Bunnell, for being one of my greatest cheerleaders and accountability partner during the writing of this book.

To my friend, Dr. Frank Page, for believing in me, for supporting me, and for the numerous times you have made my heart smile by saying "Honey, I am proud of you."

I want to sincerely thank all my family and friends who have encouraged me to keep writing. You have truly been an inspiration.

I would like to thank my friend, Ann Turner for creating the cover design. It is so exciting to work with you. You are always able to bring my vision and heart into reality.

If you love me, keep my commands. And I will ask the Father, and he will give you another advocate to help you and be with you forever-the Spirit of truth. The world cannot accept him, because it neither sees him nor knows him. But you know him, for he lives with you and will be in you. I will not leave you as orphans; I will come to you. Before long, the world will not see me anymore, but you will see me. Because I live, you also will live. On that day you will realize that I am in my Father, and you are in me, and I am in you. Whoever has my commands and keeps them is the one who loves me. The one who loves me will be loved by my Father, and I too will love them and show myself to them."

~Spoken by Jesus in
the book of John 14:15-21 NIV

The Invitation

"Now therefore, if ye will obey my voice indeed and keep my covenant, then ye shall be a peculiar treasure unto me above all people: for all the earth is mine."

Exodus 19:5

Chills! Chills! Chills! I can still remember the day God whispered His words in my ear. *"If you will obey my voice…"* Oh, the feeling that moved over my soul when the Holy Spirit spoke! I'm tearful now just typing the words. How sacred is His voice. I am wondering right now, in this moment, what kind of feelings or emotions the word obedience evokes for you. I hope it is one of beauty because nothing but beauty and blessings comes out of obedience to our God!

It was March 1, 2008 the first time Exodus 19:5 came alive to me. When the Lord guides me to a specific passage and speaks directly to me I always date it. Interesting enough, He has taken me to this same passage for three consecutive years. Each time the journey got richer and richer and looking back on it now I can see why. It was during those years God asked me to do some huge assignments. Assignments that only He could give me the strength to accomplish and by His hand I was able. It was during these years that I clung to scriptures like:"Ah Lord God! Behold, thou hast made the heaven and the earth by thy great power and stretched out arm, and there is nothing too hard for thee." Jeremiah 32:17.

Just when I thought whew! I survived! God decided to give me more assignments, and this time they were even more challenging. They would require more faith than ever before, but once again His will was accomplished. Here is what I know, God is still not done and will not be until He takes me home. There will be many more times He returns me to this passage and others that will guide me into His will. The question is, will I go? My answer is yes! I hope yours will be too. Why would anyone not want to obey the very same voice the wind and sea obey? The disciples themselves were amazed and asked, "What kind of man is this? Even the winds and waves obey him!" Matthew 8:27 NIV

To give you some history leading up to Exodus 19, the Israelites had just escaped the Red Sea. Scripture tells us that God himself took off the

Egyptians' chariot wheels that drove them so heavily towards the Israelites. Wow! I can just visualize these massive chariot wheels flying up in the air as the Lord dismantled them to protect His children. Scripture tells us in this same passage that the Egyptians themselves said "Let us flee from the face of Israel; for the Lord fighteth for them against us" Exodus 14:25. I just love this! I mean can anyone reading this get excited with me? Even our enemies run scared of the protection God provides over His children.

After Moses and the Israelites finished singing praises unto the Lord over their victory they continued to travel through the wilderness. During their travels they were persistent to complain but God was so patient with them repeatedly asking them to obey Him. In Exodus 15:26, God spoke "If thou wilt diligently hearken to the voice of the Lord thy God, and wilt do that which is right in His sight, and wilt give ear to His commandments, and keep all His statues, I will put none of these diseases upon thee, which I have brought upon the Egyptians for I am the Lord that healeth thee." Then finally, they arrived at Sinai, God's holy mountain. Scripture says in Exodus 19 verse 2 that they camped before the mount. It is here they receive the Ten Commandments, as well as instructions for building a Tabernacle for worship. It is through the Israelite's experiences at Mount Sinai we learn about the importance of obedience in our relationship with God.

Here is what happens next "And Moses went up unto God, and the Lord called unto him out of the mountain, saying, Thus shalt thou say to the house of Jacob, and tell the children of Israel; Ye have seen what I did unto the Egyptians, and how I bare you on eagles' wings, and brought you unto myself. Now therefore, if you will obey my voice indeed, and keep my covenant, then ye shall be a peculiar treasure unto me above all people: for all the earth is mine; And ye shall be unto me a kingdom of priests, and a holy nation. These are the words which thou shalt speak unto the children of Israel." Exodus 19:3-6

Wow! I love that Israel camped before the mount. I wonder how many of us just need to set up camp. Set up camp to hear from God and His directives. Mount Sinai is one of the most sacred locations in Israel's history. Located in the south-central Sinai Peninsula, this mountain is where Moses met God in a burning bush, where God makes His covenant with Israel, and where Elijah heard God in the still small voice. It is here, where God gave His people the laws and guidelines for righteous living. It is here, where they learned the potential blessings of obedience and the tragic consequences of disobedience. My favorite part of this story would be found in Exodus 19 verse 8. Moses returns to the people and spoke the words the Lord had given him. Verse 8, "And all the people answered together, and said, All that the Lord hath spoken we will do. And Moses returned the words of the people unto the Lord." They finally got it!

I knew God would have me write about obedience one day. I mean, how could He not? It is such a huge part of who I am, in Him. He has confirmed this many times, but on one particular evening after just finishing a warm bath, as I was leaning against my bed, God whispered, "*It is time.*" I headed to the computer, turned my lamp on, and there it began. Then life got busy and I hit pause. A couple of years later, I was sitting on the beach and Lord whispered, "*Be obedient, write.*" I have titled this section "Invitation" simply because an invitation can serve as a written request inviting someone to go somewhere, or to do something. I believe God is inviting YOU to go somewhere, or to do something. My prayer is that my writing inspired by God will not just be another book on obedience but rather something unique that will encourage, call, summon you to reach for God's best! God's best only comes through obedience! The greatest way to make these writings unique is to be transparent and share my own stories. I believe these stories will reach the deepest surface of your heart, because they are real and transcribed by God. They are His stories. Nothing has happened in my life that God did not use to bear fruit. Of course, first I had to surrender my heart to Him, for His will to be accomplished.

My prayer is, you will not live in a place of unbelief. Living in a place of unbelief will keep you from becoming all God purposed and created you to be. I would be so bold as to say if you are not living in obedience to God, you are living in a yoke of slavery, because walking in the obedience of God brings freedom. That is pretty radical but Jesus was radical. Jesus always obeyed the Father and He did so entirely and promptly! At times I have compromised this in my mind. I have pondered the thought maybe God does not call everyone to be as radical as I choose to be. I have had conversations with some who believed this to be true. However, I am sold out to the truth, Jesus desires all of us who receive Him as Savior, to live a life of radical obedience to Him and His great work! Why would He call you to just sit on the sidelines and not get into the game? Sitting on the sidelines is not abundant living. Scripture is clear, Jesus want us to have an abundant life abiding in Him and Him abiding in us. Jesus speaks this truth in John chapter 15, where He defines the abundant life. Abundant means full, plentiful, huge! Friends, He is all in for us and so we should be all in for Him. Nothing else makes sense.

I am sensitive to the fact that you may need deliverance. Deliverance from a person, a job, a financial matter, a place, and we could go on. I write from experience. For some of us, that could mean something small right where you are, or something larger that could require a physical relocation but know that deliverance is the action of being rescued. How beautiful! God wants to rescue you and simply guide you into His best. When God invites you to play a position in the game, sometimes you have to leave not only the people, but a place behind. This is not easy, because it may mean packing up your family and leaving behind everything you once considered comfort in your life. I understand, I have done it! I can promise you what I left behind was just a small speck compared to the greatness, vastness, and supernatural blessings that lie in front of me. As you take one step at a time, you will discover how to live a life of faith. The promise is not only will your obedience bless you, but it will bless your family, and your descendants just as it did Abraham. How about that? What a legacy, a story to leave behind!

God is the ultimate author of the story from the beginning to the end, but He gives you and I the choice. Oswald Chambers once wrote, "It is in the middle that human choices are made; the beginning and the end remain with God." Yes, it is He that must remain in the spotlight. As for me friends, I choose to follow Jesus every time. God invited me to write this book. I am choosing to do so for three reasons: First, to honor and glorify my Father, second, to empower you to follow after my Father, and third, well you guessed it, out of obedience to my Father.

When choosing to obey God it does not mean there will not be struggle. As a matter of fact many believers discover when they are determined to follow God, they immediately encounter great obstacles. The good news is you will overcome every one! If you are faithful to God He will be faithful to you. Even as I write this book, I am desperately leaning on God to help me. I run a ministry that is rapidly growing, I am a wife, and a mother of a toddler, so time is very limited. I am completely exhausted most days. So when the Lord told me it was time and I needed to get busy writing, I cried out to him, and said "Lord, How?" He simply said, *"Trust me. When you don't know what else to do just trust me."* The Holy Spirit led me to pick a day and a portion of time to honor him weekly for this assignment. I have done so and again my Lord has amazed me in how He supernaturally has provided! Each week, I am gifted with a portion of time to be alone to work. God has not only given me the strength to work, but He has given me a burst of energy, and a zeal to work. Of course, I have to also thank my husband for helping me guard this time. My point is whatever God has called you to: be obedient, walk in faith, and He will complete it.

Before I begin to seal this invitation, I want to set the stage of what is to come. God is a God of order. He has shown me through scripture when we obey Him, we obey Him in six areas which will be discussed further in the chapters ahead. These areas are: our heart, our will, our mind, our body, our finances, and our future. Notice the heart is first. I can't wait to talk to you more about the heart!

Beloved reader, I am asking you to return to Mount Sinai with me. Pull up a chair and let's set up camp and hear from God. There is no doubt in my mind that there is something contained in this book He wants you to hear. There is an exciting, blessed, promised land waiting for you if you will just listen, hear, and obey. Interesting thing about hearing, God has designed a "secret place" where He will answer and speak to you and me. We just have to be willing to go and shut the door to the outside world. This will allow us to come into His presence. He is just waiting for us. The question is, do we run to Him or just pass Him by? One day, I got a visual of the Lord anxiously waiting with such excitement for me to get up so He could spend time with me. It was one of those mornings when busy took over and I just didn't think I had time. He followed me around the house as I hurried to get ready, pour my coffee, dress my son, pack a lunch, and out the door I went. As I rushed out the door He stood there, alone, grieved, that I didn't even stop to say good morning Lord. Thank you for giving me another day. His heart was grieved because He loves me so. As I thought of this vision my heart became grieved also. What a loss I was encountering, missing the voice and presence of my Lord. There is nothing more extraordinary and satisfying to me than hearing His voice!

"He who has ears to hear, let him hear"
Matthew 13:9. NKJV.

    A point not to be missed is God was pursing the Israelites, particularly Moses, through the events in the book of Exodus. God wanted an intimate relationship that was real and personal. We do not naturally seek God. No, God seeks us. Everything we experience from God is in response to His invitation to us. God took the lead in inviting Moses into a personal relationship with Him. Time and time again He invited Moses to talk with Him and to be with Him. When Moses accepted the invitation, God then nurtured and maintained a growing relationship with Moses. It was based on love and obedience. I have learned this relationship with God is the most important factor in knowing and doing the will of God. If your love relationship with God is not as it should be, nothing else will be in order. God wants us to love Him with all of our being, energy, and soul.

    The same is true for us as it was for Moses. If we accept the invitation, He will replace our agenda with His. He is faithful to lead us from being self-centered to God-centered. Through this process a miracle happens. Our life is not the same. We become Kingdom focused. We begin to taste Heaven on earth. We begin to experience supernatural providence and witness supernatural events. The desires of our heart begin to change. He aligns our desires with His desires, and then He makes our plans succeed as in Psalm 20:4. How awesome is that! It has been so true for my own life.

Of course, the greatest invitation, the greatest news, is Jesus Christ. Above anything else I will share in this book, this is the most important. Because of God's great love for us He sent His only son, Jesus into this world to be a witness, to be sacrificed, to die, so anyone who calls upon Him and receives Him as Savior will be forgiven and granted eternal life. I can't assume because you have picked up a book like this to read, that you have already accepted this special invitation. Therefore, right now, this moment, before we go any further I want to give you the opportunity. With childlike faith simply pray:

THE INVITATION

Dear Lord Jesus,

I acknowledge that I am a sinner. I humbly ask for Your forgiveness. I believe with all my heart that you died for my sins and God raised you from the dead (Romans 10:9). At this moment, I turn away from my sins and invite you to come into my life and rule over my heart. I will follow you.

In Jesus' name, Amen!

It's intriguing how much power we have with our tongues. We can speak life or death. As Christians, in regards to obedience and the required skill to be able to listen, Bob Sorge, author of "<u>Secrets of the Secret Place</u>" spoke these words, "things don't change when I talk to God; things change when God talks to me." This is so important to capture because in order to be obedient you first have to know that God desires to speak to you. You have to hear him speak before you can act upon His Word. So my friends, position yourself to listen and hear and once you have heard, go do!

"And he took the book of the covenant, and read in the audience of the people; and they said, All that the Lord hath said will we do, and be obedient."

Exodus 24:7

Chapter 1

Shattered into Beautiful: The Heart

"If ye abide in me, and my words abide in you, ye shall ask what ye will, and it shall be done unto you."

John 15:7

It was a Sunday in 2008, when I sluggishly walked into a church in beautiful Greenville, South Carolina. Prior to this pivotal time in my life, I had been battling severe depression that was destroying my marriage. Most days I couldn't put one foot in front of the other. Typically, by 2:30 in the afternoon I was lying in bed as if it were bedtime. Doctors were concerned, believing that I was suicidal; and in all honesty I had such thoughts.

Where was all this coming from? That was the question. The previous three years had brought much disappointment as my husband and I were trying to conceive. Each month, revealed a negative test. My desperation led to fertility treatments, which were very hard emotionally and might I add unsuccessful. My last day with the fertility clinic was the day my doctor said: "Jeannie, I am sorry the treatments are just not working. At this time, we are diagnosing you with unknown infertility."

As he continued to talk, his voice grew dimmer, but I do recall something about some other treatments we could try. I thanked him for all he had done but silently knew I would not be back. I couldn't take any more. I knew if God wanted me to have a child, He was able, and He would have to do it. This marked the beginning of a long journey of learning to let go and trust God with the desires of my heart. It also marked the beginning of some darker days for me. It was in this season of life when the present desires of my heart would collide with the mistakes of my past and cause a train wreck.

The train began taking a dangerous route in 1993. It was the year I found myself in an unplanned pregnancy. Lies were spoken to me and I believed them. I didn't have the guidance I needed. I leaned on the advice of a friend, and an abortion clinic. Sadly, I chose abortion and it devastated my life. I attempted to heal the pain in my life with drugs, alcohol, and male companionship, but nothing worked. It wasn't until I sat alone in my tears, that Jesus reached down, and touched me. It was then I began to recall things from my early childhood, like kneeling beside the bed with my grandmother. I can still remember the smell of those clean sheets that I would bury my little nose in as she taught me how to pray.

It was during this time of remembrance that Jesus knocked on the door of my heart to come in, and I received Him as my Savior. It was such a joyous night, and in that moment things begin to change. Soon I was baptized, and got involved in a great local church. I was so hungry to know Jesus more. I knew God had forgiven me, but the thoughts and pain of the abortion remained.

In 2005, I married my husband. We immediately began trying to conceive but were unsuccessful. Now here I was 12 years after the abortion, wanting a child so badly, but could not have one. It caused the abortion to resurface in an ugly way. The enemy was trying to destroy me with the reminders of my past. He would whisper to me, "you had a baby:

look what you did with that one. He will not give you another. You're cursed." I began to believe the lies. I believed I was cursed. My depression got worse, my marriage was dying. I spent most days finding a place to hide, like my closet, so I could cry. Of course, no one knew my internal struggles. No one but my husband. I couldn't tell anyone. I mean, what would the church members think? I was very involved in ministry and leading small groups. Surely, this would disqualify me.

All my husband could do was pray. He prayed specifically that God would send help for his wife.

Yes, it was that morning in church, God answered my husbands' prayer. As I walked through the french doors, a bulletin was placed in my hand. As worship proceeded all around me, I opened the bulletin. It was there I read, "volunteers needed" for the local pregnancy crisis center. I did not know what a pregnancy crisis center was, but I was so drawn to the bulletin I tucked it in my Bible. Later that day, I shared it with my husband, and researched online the services provided by the organization. I quickly learned it was a ministry that helped women facing unplanned pregnancies. They offered free pregnancy testing, counsel, ultrasounds, and abortion recovery.

My husband, Carter, said "Call them! This may be what you need to help you with your pain." He also reminded me that I had been gifted flexibility in my work schedule that would afford me the opportunity to volunteer.

The next day I called. God was orchestrating it all; I just had no clue. One thing led to the next and soon I was being interviewed for a volunteer position. Her name was Tami. She was so kind. She asked me the question, "Have you ever had an abortion?" It was foreign to me, but for the first time since my abortion I felt safe. Safe to answer her truthfully, "Yes, I have." Next, she asked, "Have you ever received God's healing?" This question left me a little uncertain. She continued on, telling me that if I wanted to be a volunteer it was a requirement for all post-abortion women to attend their post-abortion Bible study. I told her I would consider it. I went home and shared this with my husband, who was all for me attending the Bible study. I was reluctant, and there arose the question from the Lord, *"Will you go? Obey my voice."* The decision was made, "Yes Lord, I will go."

Oh I'm so thankful, so thankful God led me to that Bible study! I was in real need, and the result of my obedience was a changed life! It changed my marriage! Yes, I had been forgiven, but I had not had the opportunity to heal. I learned there was a difference.

During this study, I was able to safely grieve and honor my child, now in heaven. The Bible study came to completion in May 2009. It was a miracle in my life and I was so thankful! I became a volunteer and began serving at the pregnancy center. One day I got a call from Dana, my center director. After our sweet hellos, she began to tell me there was a need and she believed the Lord wanted me to meet it. There was an upcoming fundraising banquet for the center, and the woman chosen to give her testimony had an emergency and was not able to attend. She asked, "Jeannie, would you consider being the testimony?"

I could barely swallow. Fear began to overtake me and the phone became silent. I loved Dana; she had spoken so much encouragement into my life so I did not want to disappoint her, but I just didn't think I could do this. I had just finished the Bible study: it was all so new to me. Only a few people knew of my abortion, and now she was suggesting I get up publicly and share it with strangers at a fundraising banquet? Then came the still, sweet voice, "Jeannie are you there?" I replied, "Yes Dana,

I am here. Can I pray about this and call you back?" She responded once more, "Yes, of course." After hanging up the phone, I began to tell God I could not do this. Then the question from God flooded my soul again, *"Will you go? If you will obey my voice…"* I knew what I had to do. I called Dana back and told her yes, I would do it. The next day, they called and asked my husband to join me and share how the experience affected him and our marriage.

The night of the banquet I was so nervous I couldn't even eat, but there was still an inner peace that flowed in me. I carried in my hand all night a rock I had been given the last day of our Bible study. I know that may sound strange, but this rock represented the stone Samuel took and named Ebenezer, claiming the Lord has helped from 1 Samuel 7:12-13. It signified the Lord's faithfulness. So when our names were called to approach the stage, I clenched the rock no one could see tightly in my hand and took one step after the next forward.

That night my husband and I gave our testimony for the first time in front of 1200 people. As we finished, the guests stood and applauded our courage. No rocks came from the back of the room only applause. God was faithful. I had trusted Him with my heart and He was faithful. I was so happy. We made our way back to our seats, I released the rock from my sweaty palm, and finally I could eat.

The next day I was in prayer, thanking the Lord for what He had done in my life. He sent His word to heal me and saved me from my destruction (Psalm 107:20). I was face down, stretched on the floor in tears, saying, "Lord, for what you have done for me I surrender my life to you." It is hard to put into words the joy that overtook my soul during those moments, but I knew my offering had been accepted. I continued, "Use me Lord, and show me how to serve you." Well, I had no idea what lie ahead for me, but that particular day I so clearly heard Him say, *"Write."*

Now, I love to write. I have a passion for reading and writing and for putting words together that express my heart. When the Lord told me to write, it was nothing new to me. There were many things I had written: devotionals, articles, and I once attended She Speaks Conference, a ministry of Proverbs 31, and presented a book proposal. However, this was different, and I knew it. There was something very specific God wanted me to write about.

The same day He spoke giving me my assignment, I pressed into His Word, seeking the subject

He wanted me to write about. Then it came. He wanted me to write about my abortion. My abortion! "Oh Lord," I pleaded, "what about some of the other things you have led me to write?" He whispered, *"No my child, everything else you have written, the opportunities you have been given, have been used to equip and prepare you for this assignment."* I tried to bargain with God. As if I knew what was best, but I knew the rubber was meeting the road and there it was again, *"If you will obey my voice…"*

At that moment, I had a decision to make. I had just poured out my heart in thanksgiving and offered to follow after Him. God searches for the hearts of those who will surrender and obey Him at all cost. My heart was genuine in my offering. He knew that. My only option was to obey and obey with a grateful heart. I was up for the job, but I pondered on how in the world it would all happen. God began to supernaturally do things. He would drop names in my spirit, guide my conversations, and before I knew it I was signing a book contract on March 3, 2010. I sat down with the Lord and made a plan. He was only calling me to do my part and He would take care of the rest. So, I carved out time each week to show up and write, and by His great works, all other details fell into place.

To my surprise, as I was working on this assignment, the Lord brought another opportunity. The pregnancy center that ministered to me, and where I was now volunteering was working on a post-abortive film. This film would share God's healing through script and testimonies. My husband and I were asked to be one of the testimonies in the film titled, *"Set Free."* Again the Lord spoke, and I chose obedience. During the filming, the producers asked to return to our home to do some additional filming. We didn't understand why but we obeyed. I was asked to play out parts of my story. They called it B-rolls. In October 2010, the film was complete and released. When it was released we were completely shocked and humbled. They had chosen our story to be the lead testimony. We were so honored to play a part in this great work of God. I could not believe what all God was doing! It took me a year to complete the book, and what a journey it was! Each week as I met with God and wrote, I was inspired by His presence. He was courting me, and it felt as if He was healing me all over again, but at a deeper level. God was faithful, and as a result of my obedience, on March 15, 2011, I held in my hands the first copy in print of my book, <u>"Shattered into Beautiful: Delivering the Brokenhearted from Abortion."</u>

There had been a major shift in my life. My relationship with the Lord had completely changed. I wondered if others around me were experiencing God in the way I was experiencing Him. I hoped so, but I was learning a relationship like this only springs forth through obedience. There was a bounce in my step, a light shining from within, a permanent smile on my face. It was one thing to read and study about Him, but when God turned my ashes to beauty, when He made me clean and whole, when He moved mountains on my behalf, life was never the same. He had done so much in just two years' time. I wanted to do nothing else but be obedient to all He called me to do. It was my greatest desire. God was so faithful to speak to me through the Holy Spirit, His Word, and others. I giggle even now as I recall a visit with some friends. They are graphic designers, but also just a godly couple who offer their talents for kingdom work. I knew the Lord wanted me to visit with them, but I thought it was to have them create an envelope design for me. Turns out, God used them to open my eyes to a greater vision He was calling me to.

I discovered a quote during this season of my life that became a favorite. It was from Hudson Taylor. He said, "I have found there are three stages in every great work of God. First, it is impossible, then it is difficult, then it is done." I related to his words in such a personal way. They ministered to me, and I was intrigued to learn more about the man who wrote them. I studied Hudson Taylor's life. I was inspired even more by his life. He was a missionary who had a calling for China. In many ways, Hudson Taylor and I have gone through similar journeys with the Lord. I knew that when I read a journal entry he wrote very similar to my own journal entry. In Hudson Taylor's, "_Spiritual Secret_" it reads:

"Well do I remember how in the gladness of my heart I poured out my soul before God. Again and again confessing my grateful love to Him who had done everything for me, who had saved me when I had given up all hope and even desire for salvation. I besought Him to give me some work to do for Him as an outlet for love and gratitude… Well do I remember as I put myself, my life, my friends, my all upon the altar, the deep solemnity that came over my soul with the assurance that my offering was accepted. The presence of God became unutterably real and blessed, and I remember…stretching myself on the ground and lying before Him with unspeakable awe and unspeakable joy. For what service I was accepted I knew not, but a deep consciousness that I was not my own took possession of me which has never since been effaced."

I have experienced the words of Hudson Taylor. My prayer is that you will too. We are not all called to be great missionaries in China, but if we are willing, God will call us to something. He will use us for some great work. He may call you to be obedient to lead a Bible study in your neighborhood, lead a mission trip in your church, plant a church, work in the church nursery, or feed the hungry. God's work cannot be measured, my friend, because every work of God is a great work!

Please open your heart, listen to the Lord as we work through this book together. I will share with you more stories that will encourage you along the way, but it will be God who speaks to your heart. How will your heart respond?

God is more concerned with our heart than anything else. Let me tell you why. The heart is a Biblical word used to describe who and what we are at the deepest level of our very existence. Out of the heart rises up all our relationships and responses to those relationships, God, and life itself. It is the core of our personality. A place we do business with God, either living in obedience with Him or in rebellion against Him. Did you catch that? If we are not in obedience with Him, we are not only in rebellion but are working against Him. Overall, the heart is the chief source of our total behavior. This should leave it no surprise; the subject of the heart is the most important to God.

God is so amazing, even in the way He created our hearts. By career, as a health care professional, I can tell you the heart is the most vital organ in our whole body. It is beating in our chest dispersing blood through our veins and arteries flowing oxygen and nutrients necessary for us to live. It sustains our life which makes it the source of our physical life. What the physical heart is to our physical life, so is the spiritual heart to our spiritual life. I really admire just like the physical heart, which is divided into four chambers, the Biblical explanation of the heart may be understood as four chambers. The heart promotes our personality functions from a spiritual, intellectual, emotional, and volitional state. In combination, this could be said to reveal one's true character and nature. Don't just take my words on it; let's look at it from a scriptural point of view.

Spiritually the heart:
Prays Genesis 24:45, 1 Samuel 1:13, **Responds to God** II Kings 22:19, **Sings to God** Psalm 30:12, **Seeks God** Deuteronomy 4:29, Psalm 119:2,10, **Believes** Romans 10:9-10, **Pure** Psalm 24:4, Matthew 5:8.

Intellectually the heart:
Thinks Mark 2:8, Genesis 6:5, Luke 5:22, **Understands** Proverbs 2:2, **Has Wisdom and Knowledge** Proverbs 2:10, **Acknowledge**s Deuteronomy 4:39, **Doubts** Mark 11:23, **Lays Up Words** Job 22:22

Emotionally the heart:
Angry Psalm 39:3, **Discouraged** Joshua 2:11, **Delighted** Ecclesiastes 2:10, Jeremiah 15:16, **Anguished** Isaiah 64:14, Romans 9:2, **Heavy** Proverbs 25:20

Volitionally the heart:
Decides II Chronicles 6:7, II Chronicles 9:7, **Yields** Joshua 24:23, **Directs** II Thessalonians, **Desires** Romans 10:1, Psalm 21:2, **Does** According to Itself I Samuel 2:35

In a physical and spiritual way, the heart can get out of rhythm. Physically when this happens it can be life threatening. Wouldn't the same apply spiritually? I think we all get out of rhythm at times. It is the battle we are in, and there is nothing the enemy wants more than to take us off course and navigate us away from the center of God's will for our lives. We must believe this and stay on guard, which brings me to my next point.

There are two kinds of hearts. A believing heart and an unbelieving heart. It's important to know even as a Christian we can have an unbelieving heart. An unbelieving heart is blinded by the god of this world and does not respond in faith. For example, in my post-abortion experience, I was a Christian but I did not believe God could do anything about my pain. It was when I began to believe and trust God with my pain that a miracle happened in my life. It was when my believing heart partnered up with faith that things began to happen. He gave me a new heart and a new spirit! He rocked my world! He became my personal Savior because He met my personal needs. No one can do that but God! It changed my entire relationship and outlook on Him as my Savior.

What do you need to believe God for right now?

I want you to reposition yourself and your heart to receive all God wants to give you. Yes! This could be the best things that ever happen to you. Don't miss it and don't believe the lies. Jesus is Truth. Anything apart from Jesus is a lie. There is a progression strategy the enemy uses. It starts with deception and leads to bondage. Let me detail this out for you.

First, we listen to the lie (deception, seed planted) = false input.

Second, we dwell on the lie (fertilized and watered) = consider input.

Third, we believe the lie (sown, takes root) = growth of input.

Fourth, we act on the lie (seed produces fruit) = production of input.

Now we have a false belief system that is producing behavior. Know that every act of sin in our lives begins with a lie. This is important when it comes to obedience, because if you are believing the lies the enemy speaks to you, it may defeat the courage to move forward in what God has prepared for you. There is no doubt He has a gift to give you. Let's unwrap it!

I love John chapter 15. It is probably one of my most favorite chapters in the Bible. It is in this chapter Jesus teaches about the vine and the branches. In my opinion, it is the secret to life. It is here we discover some truth about obedience and see Jesus's own obedience to the Father. As I end this chapter with His chosen words, may your heart be shattered into beautiful from this day forward over His love for you. May you discover that obedience leads to joy, and may you realize He is the greatest friend you will ever have.

"As the Father hath loved me, so have I loved you: continue ye in my love. If you keep my commandments, ye shall abide in my love even as I have kept my Father's commandments, and abide in his love. These things have I spoken unto you, that my joy might remain in you, and that your joy might be full. This is my commandment, that ye love one another, as I have loved you. Greater love hath no man than this that a man lay down his life for his friends. Ye are my friends, if ye do whatsoever I command you. Henceforth I call you not servants; for the servants knoweth not what his lord doeth: but I have called you friends; for all things that I have heard of my Father I have made known unto you. Ye have not chosen me, but I have chosen you, and ordained you, that ye should go and bring forth fruit, and that your fruit should remain: that whatsoever ye shall ask of the Father in my name, he may give it to you."

John 15: 9-16

IF YOU LOVE ME OBEY ME

Chapter 2

The Scary Unknown: OUR WILL

"Also I heard the voice of the Lord, saying, whom shall I send, and who will go for us? Then said I, Here am I; send me."

Isaiah 6:8

There I sat in my favorite place, staring out the window as the sun glistened off the beautiful crepe myrtle tree in my front yard. I had positioned and planted the tree so I could look at it each day as it grew to its greatest potential. I was looking forward to watching it grow from the window of our beautiful newly built home in Greenville, South Carolina. I never dreamed of living in such a place. I could walk out the front door and see green pastures, or the back and see mountain tops.

But this particular morning was different than the others. It was there that morning as I nestled into my favorite place, into my routine time with God that He whispered, *"Will you go?"*

Go! Go where? I didn't understand. We just got settled here! I wrestled with God. Why would He ask me to leave? I reminded God of how wonderful everything was going here. I was continuing to serve at the pregnancy center, my husband and I were co-facilitating a young married class at church, my husband's career was soaring, we had great friends, and loved our community. We were making a difference here! Why would we leave?

As much as I wrestled, I could not deny what I was hearing. During my quiet time with the Lord this particular morning the call was so clear and defined. He even directed the location He was sending us and for what purpose. As the Lord was speaking, I was journaling as fast as I could what I was hearing. Once it was done, I sat back in my chair, reflected upon what I wrote, and slammed my journal shut in rebellion. No, I thought, that is not happening! As much as I wanted to fight it, the truth was as God spoke that morning He was already beginning to detach my heart from my home, my surroundings, the area, and the community I had come to love. It just didn't make any sense to me. So many good things were happening. In my opinion, God was just getting started where we were at. Why would He send us away?

I had so many questions. Then in the quiet God spoke to my heart. He gently reminded me of the moment when I fell on my face before Him and cried out, "God for what you have done for me I will do whatever you call me to do." It was then in my humility that I opened back up the journal I had slammed shut and embraced what God had spoken on this day. There it was written on May 4th, 2011, "God is sending me to Myrtle Beach, South Carolina to start a pregnancy crisis center."

I didn't know what to do with this information. This is not the plan I had for my life. This is not how I thought God was going to use me. I didn't know how to share this heavenly yet scary directive with my husband, so I just didn't. I pondered it in my heart for a few days. I knew God would have to prepare my husband's heart and speak to him as well, so I waited on God. In the meantime, I knew God was calling me into ministry. I had spent years asking God during my journaling time, "God what is my ministry?" I now had clarity on what it was, and it was evident God did not want part of me:

He wanted all of me. I knew He was calling me to step down from my career as a physical therapist assistant and to trust Him now with my future and kingdom purpose.

Soon, I shared this revelation with my husband, who completely supported the decision for me to resign. His next response was, "Jeannie, we need to sell the house." What! but when I settled down it did not surprise me for two reasons: First, as beautiful as our home was, as I much as I enjoyed it, it never really felt like home. I had spent a small fortune trying to make it feel so, but I was never successful. Now it made sense to me. God never intended for it to be our final destination. Second, I knew God had spoken to my husband in reference to what He spoke to me the day of my journaling. We were leaving, and the process had begun.

This all happened during a time when our house should not have sold. The market had bottomed out. Nothing was selling, and no one was buying. Against all odds, we hired an agent and placed the For Sale sign in the front yard, right in front of my beautiful crepe myrtle. In all honesty it was a sad time. Our neighbors along with myself spent may days in tears. We had developed such strong relationships with them, and God had used us to minister to them in many ways. No one understood, including us, but we knew we were walking out God's will for our lives.

The following Sunday, we sat down with our co-facilitators from Sunday school. We loved and respected them dearly and we knew we needed to tell them what God was doing in our life. We shared the call on our lives with them and asked them to pray as we tried to be obedient to God's leading. Each day we waited on God, each day we clung to His word and sought Him through prayer in what to do next. We were being obedient, and the results were up to Him.

Within three months, August 2011, we had received the full asking price offer on our home and a closing date. Our agent was shocked this would happen considering the market at the time, but my husband and I knew it was the movement of God. It was more confirmation. We knew God was not ready to send us out of the area yet, so we began searching for a holding place. We prayerfully decided upon an apartment complex close to my husband's office. It was a two-bedroom unit with a large office, which would allow me the space to work and continue homeschooling my stepson. It also provided a storage unit to hold all our belongings.

It was perfect. Now we needed to decide upon the lease term. There were many options. As we prayed God continued to give us the number eight. So we signed an eight-month lease to begin the date of our closing. This would have our lease ending the following year, April 2012. This was significant because we knew that during this eight-month time frame God would complete His work through us in Greenville, while preparing the foundation of where He was sending us. It would be a time of both ending and beginning.

Before we knew it, we were pulling out of the neighborhood we came to love in a moving truck headed to our new destination. At times it was as if I was in a dream. I could not believe what was happening and the speed in which it was happening. But as we pulled out, I looked back, and to my surprise I did not feel sadness, but joy for what was mysteriously ahead. It was if God had completely closed the door to that chapter of our life. All we had moving forward were fond memories.

During the next eight months, God was doing a work. I listened passionately as He directed my every move. Repeatedly we sought confirmation. I talked to different organizations in the area He was sending us to confirm the need God was showing me. I discovered there had never been a pregnancy crisis center in the entire county. I was shocked because I knew there was a great need. I studied maps and surrounding areas. Geographically, the county was the largest ground county in our state offering no hope or assistance to those facing an unplanned pregnancy. We made several trips to the area just to pray and requested others to pray. God gave me wisdom, He gave me mentors, and it was in that apartment He birthed the vision of the ministry in which He was calling me to. He gave me a name, a location, even colors. I could see it all. During those eight months, my roles were a wife, homeschooling mom, and a founder of a new ministry. I could handle the first two, but the third one was completely out of my comfort zone, as I learned what was required to fulfil this role. I had never written a business plan or filed paper work for a nonprofit. I had not a clue, and interesting enough, as I tried my best to find help and lean on others to help me, God closed every door. He made it clear to me that I was not to lean on anyone but Him. He alone would be my teacher and would complete His perfect will in me. So the work began.

There were three principles I clung to during this time, and they came from the book of Habakkuk.

This is a small book consisting of only three chapters, but oh so powerful and full of wisdom. It is a great book to refer to when experiencing doubt, because it instructs us how to reject doubt and instead seek God for answers. Even today as I write this, God has returned me to these same truths as I am walking through this particular season of my life. Habakkuk was a prophet, and such a man! Habakkuk's questions and God's answers are recorded in this book. The importance of the book is that Habakkuk responded in faith. In chapter two, God instructed Habakkuk to do three things: watch, write, and wait. I have recorded it here for you.

"I will stand upon my watch, and set me upon the tower, and will watch to see what he will say unto me, and what I shall answer when I am reproved. And the Lord answered me, and said, write the vision, and make it plain upon tables, that he may run that readeth it. For the vision is yet for an appointed time, but at the end it shall speak, and not lie: though it tarry, wait for it; because it will surely come, it will not tarry. Behold, his soul which is lifted up is not upright in him: but the just shall live by his faith." Habakkuk 2:1-4

So I watched, I wrote, and I waited. Every day

the Lord was faithful to give insight, instruction, and inspiration. My only job was to be obedient. During this time, I was still volunteering at the local pregnancy crisis center. I was continuing to serve as a counselor and had just finished my training to serve as an abortion recovery facilitator. The Lord was prompting me to inform the leadership of the pregnancy center, I had come to love, of His work in me. I was so saddened at the thought of leaving them. After all my service and training, was I not going to be able to lead one woman through abortion recovery in this beautiful ministry? I was obedient, and I sent a formal letter to the pregnancy crisis center, explaining God was calling my family away to serve Him, and although we were not certain what this calling fully looked like, we knew we would soon be leaving. I expressed my love for them and gratitude for all they had done to minister to me and my family. Of course, I let them know I would continue to serve them and those hurting until our departure.

God was so good to give me the desire of my heart. Soon after, I got a call from the abortion recovery team at the center. They asked me if I would be willing to lead a young woman through the abortion recovery Bible study before I left.

The young woman had a unique story, and I knew God had purposed me to lead her to healing. He also purposed the timing. She would be leaving to go into the navy early spring just along the same time as our lease would be up and we would be headed out to the unknown. I knew this was the last assignment God would give me in beautiful Greenville, South Carolina.

As I was busy facilitating abortion recovery and following the three principles spelled out in Habakkuk, God was continuing to do a work in my husband. My husband is a nurse and served as Executive Director for a highly respected hospice organization in the community. Under his leadership, the branch reached its highest achievements ever, and I really believe it was because my husband honored God in that place. Hospice was a ministry to him. He inspired his staff with his own faith as he encouraged the importance of the love of Christ to be shared during the end stages of life to all those encountered. What we quickly began to see was how God had woven the passion of life into the fabric of my husband's heart. It was during his service in hospice that he developed a love and passion for life in a new way from the beginning of conception until one's last breath.

THE SCARRY UNKNOWN: OUR WILL

I will never forget the day he walked in from work and announced to me that he met with his regional supervisor and informed her that he would be resigning soon and moving to the coast to serve God in ministry. My response was "What!" I went on to explain to him that we had not discussed this and God had not given the directive of his resignation yet. He then went on to tell me, "Yes, God did. He gave me the directive." Well there you go. The last thing holding us to the area was my husband's great job that financially provided so well for my family. I knew that day God's work in my husband's heart had been done. He was willing to abandon even his career that he had worked so hard to build. During this time, there was a magnificent work being done in both of us. We viewed everything differently than we ever had before; our desires had changed, and our motives had changed. Most importantly, our will had changed.

Our will had aligned with the Father's will, and it began to feel like nothing else mattered anymore. Of course, the company did not want to lose my husband so they attempted to figure out a way to keep him employed. We were willing to entertain some ideas, but our mind and heart was set on the will and work of God. We didn't know what the future held, but surprisingly enough we were not concerned about it. I wish I could say the same about our family and friends. I can tell you that during this season of life many of them thought we were absolutely nuts. They asked questions we simply could not answer because we didn't know ourselves. To the world it made no sense to lay down two great careers to follow after the unknown, but to us it was the only thing that made any sense, and we knew our Father was pleased so we were at total peace.

As I studied scripture concerning obedience, I learned that it was a process like most everything else. In this chapter we are focusing on the will. When we seek to be obedient to God, we have to understand there is a commitment and a surrender. God gives us free will. There are several passages in scripture that teach us this principle. Proverbs 16:9 says "The heart of man plans his way, but the Lord establishes his steps."ESV God allows us to choose. Joshua 24:15 says "…choose this day whom you will serve…"

We are talking about two different wills. To fully understand this, we must understand flesh versus Spirit. In Galatians 5:16-17 ESV it says "But I say, walk by the Spirit, and you shall not gratify the desires of the flesh. For the desires of the flesh are against the Spirit, and the desires of the Spirit are against the flesh, for these are opposed to each other, to keep you from doing the things you want to do." So, bottom line we either walk in the flesh or we walk in the Spirit. That's it! Plain and simple.

Prior to receiving Christ as Savior, I walked in the flesh. As I walked in the flesh, I lived in a place of bondage because my sin had dominion over me. God gave me a choice to remain in the flesh or receive His son Jesus as Savior and begin walking in the Spirit, which I did. Now on the contrary, after being born again in the Spirit, I now had dominion over my sin because of the power of the Holy Spirit residing in me. Now I am equipped with the power to overcome the sin. Paul tells us in 1 Corinthians 10:13 that "No temptation has overtaken you that is not common to man. God is faithful, and He will not let you be tempted beyond your ability, but with the temptation He will also provide the way of escape, that you may be able to endure it."

Once receiving this great gift, our life is not our own anymore. We are now heirs with Jesus Christ and adopted into God's family (Romans 8:17). The thought just leaves me speechless because I am so undeserving. Yes! We are heirs of God's glory! In

Matthew chapter 6, Jesus taught the disciples how to pray. He said "Our Father, which art in Heaven, hollowed be thy name. Thy kingdom come, thy will be done..." And so it is we must choose to align our will with His will. Once we surrender, God is so faithful to teach us His will. This is what the Lord says – your Redeemer, the Holy One of Israel: "I am the Lord your God, who teaches you what is best for you, who directs you in the way you should go." Isaiah 48:17. NIV

Looking back on it all now, I can tell you, I never dreamed God would do all the great things He has done. During that time, God only showed me glimpses, because my mind could have never comprehended the magnitude of what He had planned. But friends, what I can tell you in full confidence is God's will is so much better than our will, and If we truly love Him, we are not just eager, but excited to jump on board. How about we allow God's deliverance to move us right into a full calendar of His events that will impact all the way to Glory!

THE SCARRY UNKNOWN: OUR WILL

Jesus said to them,

"truly I tell you, at the renewal of all things, when the Son of Man sits on his glorious throne, you who have followed me will also sit on twelve thrones, judging the twelve tribes of Israel. And everyone who has left houses or brothers or sisters or father or mother or wife or children or fields for My sake will receive a hundred times as much and will inherit eternal life."

Matthew 19:28-29 NIV

Wow! Did you feel those chills?

IF YOU LOVE ME OBEY ME

Chapter 3

Time for Battle: OUR MIND

"Casting down imaginations, and every high thing that exalteth itself against the knowledge of God, and bringing into captivity every thought to the obedience of Christ."

2 Corinthians 10:5

The day had come. I watched as the moving truck backed into our apartment complex to begin the loading. It was pouring rain outside. My husband had suddenly developed the flu and could barely climb the steps leading to our door. At one point, I found him lying face down on a mattress while the employees of the moving company escorted our belongings from the only home we had known for the last eight months. There were all sorts of emotions racing within me. Some I could mask and some I could not. I still today can envision a moment when we were standing in an empty living room. Our two dogs were lying together on their bed shaking and my stepson was sitting in a corner. I leaned up against the wall. I began to slide down into a seated position to join him, when my phone rang. It was the manager from the apartment complex in Myrtle Beach. She was calling to let me know there was a problem with the apartment we had leased. She began to tell me when the painters went in to paint an accent wall they were attacked by fleas and discovered the apartment was flea infested. What! I replied. She went on to tell me there was not another apartment available to lease at this time. She had checked all their other facilities and they were completely full as well. The phone went silent. Finally, she spoke and I heard the words "I'm so sorry."

Sorry! Sorry! That's it, I'm sorry. I stood there frazzled repeating the words silently in my head. I asked, "What are we going to do?" My husband quickly told me to call our lease manager and explain what happened. Our hope was an unleased furnished apartment we could move into until we figured out what to do next. The answer was, they did not. In fact, they had already leased our apartment and she informed me so graciously we had to be out that day so housekeeping could come in. My husband and I began to brain storm ideas of what to do next. We knew we had friends that would welcome us in. It was really the only option for us if we were going to stay put in Greenville while we worked through the situation, but the possibility of it just did not feel right to us. At that moment, one of the kind men moving our furniture stepped back in the doorway to let me know the last load they took down would not fit on the truck. He stated he was sorry, but they estimated the wrong size truck. He went on to tell me they located a larger truck but they would have to charge us labor to unload and load again. He then asked me if we could rent a storage unit and come back at another time to get the rest. I could not believe everything that was happening.

It was obstacle after obstacle. The rain was coming down harder. Some of our furniture was getting soaked and potentially ruined. Suddenly, there was a battle going on in my head. All the obstacles were beginning to make things seem impossible. With all the struggle, I began to wonder if we were doing the right thing. I began to question if we really heard from God. I was in complete distress. Mentally, I was replaying everything in my mind. I desperately needed to hear from God! Just one more time. I needed some solid confirmation. I looked around and noticed that everything was loaded on the truck except for my desk remaining in the office where God had birthed this ministry in my heart. Without telling anyone, with a heavy heart, I took one step at a time until I reached the desk. There was a window above the desk. I saw nothing in sight but rain. It felt like time had stopped. I dropped my head in despair and began to cry out to God. I prayed, "Lord, please confirm we are doing the right thing. I need you right now Lord." At that divine moment as I lifted my head, and looked out the window a big yellow truck went by. Down the side of the truck was one word…MOVING. In a blink of an eye it was gone. I had never seen a moving truck like it before and haven't still to this day but one thing I knew for sure God had spoken and it was time to get rolling.

Suddenly, the rain stopped. Then we received another blessing. The apartment manager agreed to let us use one of their storage units for the rest of our furniture that would not fit on the truck until we could come back and get it. There are two more things I remember about our departure that day. The first, is a visit filled with tears from one of my best friends. She had come to see us off bringing a gift of my favorite homemade bread. The second, was the comical view of both our dogs sitting in the passenger seat of the moving truck with their heads out the window as my husband drove out the gates. They looked confused and had no idea where we were going. Well, neither did we.

All we knew to do was drive. So we just drove towards our destination. It was getting late in the day and we were exhausted. We decided to make a pit stop at my husband's parents' house. Their home was half way to where we knew we needed to go. We called and told them we were coming but gave no other details. Once we got there and explained what had happened their response was for us to live with them until we found another apartment. The thought of it sounded comforting to me and honestly I was all for it. However, my husband quickly responded and said "thank you for the offer, but tomorrow morning we are leaving for the area God called us to. We have to trust He has gone before us to prepare the way. We have to trust

He will take care of us." There was nothing less than confidence in his voice so I followed his lead.

The next morning, we drove straight into the unknown. We knew no one in the area and knew not where to go. As we were driving, I got a call from the apartment manager. She called to tell me she found us an apartment. In desperation, I leased it over the phone and then called my mom and asked her to drive to South Carolina to help us unload and get settled. Once we all got there we quickly realized the apartment was not feasible. It was so small. The doorways would not even allow our furniture to pass through. It was not going to work. I could not believe it, but we were stranded again. The apartment manager was kind enough to release us from the agreement. On the search again, we parked our moving truck in a department store parking lot and used our other vehicle to search for an apartment. There was nothing. Nothing was available to accommodate our needs. We drove around all day. I will never forget the feeling of not knowing where we were going to lay our head. The fact we had three animals at the time was making any chance of anything difficult. We were getting weary and finally the Lord sent a life boat. We suddenly remembered the name of a very kind real estate agent we met in the area the previous year as we were seeking God's direction in the move. I located his card and we phoned him. He told us of a "home away from home" hotel that would allow animals. I couldn't believe it. We drove there immediately and praise God they had a room. As we began to settle in we realized all our clothes were packed at the front of the moving truck. It was impossible to get to them and most of them were taped in our dresser drawers. We assumed when we packed that we would be unloading the same day. Big mistake! I will never go through a move again without packing a few days' worth of clothes and personal toiletries. That's right we could not even locate our toothbrushes. So we picked ourselves up once again and made our way to the local goodwill, and Walmart to buy some items of necessity.

During this season of life, God had strategically placed some individuals of faith in my life I was honored to call friends. These friends were there to hold my hand and cheer me on every step of the way. They would speak boldly to me and when I was so tempted to bail out they were there to lift me up and confirm my calling. They refused to let me do anything but be obedient to God. After our goodwill shopping spree, I sat in the hotel laundry room watching the clothes spin round and round. I was emotionally struggling. I cried, wanting to return to what was comfortable. I knew I needed support so I called a mentor and friend named Marsha. Marsha and her husband Dan was the couple we taught Sunday school with and whom we sat down and shared this call from God. I began to update Marsha on everything going on. I began to cry and tell her I just wanted to run, turn around, and come back to Greenville. In her gentle, sweet voice she simply said "yes, that may be what you want to do, but you know that's not the right thing to do." There was silence. Of course, I wanted her to agree and just tell me to come back but that wasn't what I heard. She was calm, nothing I told her shook her confidence in me and the calling on our family. Through her words, God gave me the fuel I needed to face another day.

So vividly I remember those next few days of searching. Searching for some place to call home. We called every apartment building, responded to every rental advertisement and still nothing. We lived there for 3 weeks before we found a home. During those three weeks, my husband was fulfilling his commitment to his employer in Greenville.

As I mentioned, they didn't want to lose him so they created a position on a corporate level. this allowed him some flexibility to work from home, but most of the time it required him to travel. As tough as it was we had to see it though. We needed the income until God provided something else, and eventually He did. Until then, we lived out of our moving truck that was parked in front of the hotel. It was packed so tight every time I rolled the door up something fell onto ground. I remember the humble feeling that came upon me when my step son asked me where we were going to live. I remember the sick feeling that came upon me when my husband had to leave us while he returned back to Greenville to work. Through it all, there was only one I could lean on to meet all my needs and His name was Jesus.

It was all a process. God was doing a great work in us all. We learned to take our eyes off the circumstances and look to Him in greater trust. I feel confident to say all the trials was a great test. A test of our obedience and trust. The Good news is we passed and God provided a wonderful town home for us to live in. It was located in one of the most desired communities. We enjoyed a summer of luxury and fun as we continued to fulfil God's will. I was very thankful.

I had to work through the battle of the mind. When God calls you the enemy is not going to just stand by. He will cause confusion, obstruction, and fear. In your mind you will try and reason. One of the greatest books I have read concerning the mind is by Joyce Meyer called *Battlefield of the Mind*. Joyce shares that reasoning leads to confusion. She states "Satan frequently steals the will of God from us due to reasoning. The Lord may direct us to do a certain thing, but if it does not make sense- if it is not logical- we may be tempted to disregard it. What God leads a person to do does not always make logical sense to his mind. His spirit may affirm it and His mind reject it, especially if it would be out of the ordinary or unpleasant or if it would require personal sacrifice or discomfort." You will be tempted to make decisions based on the circumstances instead of obedience to God. You must know that God's ways are not our ways. His timing is not our timing. Don't reason in the mind just obey the Spirit. "Trust in the Lord with all your heart, And lean not on your own understanding;" Proverbs 3:5 NIV

As I have been writing this chapter, I have experienced much spiritual warfare in my own life. I have had to strategically overcome much in my mind. Oh yes, the enemy was warring against me and certainly did not want me to share these truths with you. I walked in a state of heaviness concerning some challenges in our ministry. I was in a raging war of flesh and Spirit. My human mind tried to reason the things going on around me. It was a familiar place. I had been there before and I knew I could overcome if I would persevere. All I could do was get up each day, get dressed, and show up for work. Guess what? That is all we have to do. With the power of the Holy Spirit we will overcome any and all things the enemy plots against us. Our job is just to be a faithful servant. After days of battling, I crawled out of bed to have my quiet time with the Lord. It was that morning, down on my knees, I rose to victory! The battle was over and by the power of the Holy Spirit I won. My mind played an important role in the victory but the rewards of the victory poured out on everyone around me. My eyes were not set on my circumstances but on the Lord in my circumstances. I became rich with clarity!

That battle was over but there will be more. We win the battle in our mind by seeking to know Him and His word, so His principles and values form the foundation of all we think and do. Then we can walk peacefully as we entrust the circumstances to Him. I have learned a lot about circumstances as well. Circumstances can make you better or make you bitter. We may think if our circumstances were different we would be different but not true. Satan loves to use circumstances to attack your mind. If only I had... If only I could... oh yes I have been there too many times. The truth is, if we are not happy with our current circumstances chances are we will not be happy with a new set of circumstances. George Washington's wife expressed it this way:

"I am still determined to be cheerful and happy in whatever situation I may be; for I have also learned from experience that the greater part of our happiness or misery depends on our dispositions and not our circumstances. We carry the seeds of the one or the other about with us in our minds, wherever we go."

Wow! What wisdom. Apostle Paul said something very similar:

"I am not saying this because I am in need, for I have learned to be content whatever the circumstances. I know what it is to be in need, and I know what it is to have plenty. I have learned the secret of being content in any and every situation, whether well fed or hungry, whether living in plenty or in want." Philippians 4:11-12 (NIV)

As I wrote this chapter, I struggled with sharing the full details of my families' circumstances as we set out to do God's will. I wondered if you would even care to read them, but God would not let me rest until I reflected upon every single one. In a sense, it was like reliving it all again. Then I realized God was doing a work in me. This writing is not just for you, but for me as well. Through this assignment, I have been able to set my eyes on Him in a greater way. He has lifted my chin up a little higher. He has reminded me in every impossible situation He was there. He has never forsaken me and He will not forsake you. Maybe you're in a place where you need to be reminded of God's proven will in your life or maybe you want to know God's perfect will. You can! By simply renewing your mind.

God has perfect plans for us. As we walk out those plans, He wants us to have renewed minds. Minds that seek to honor and obey Him. Our minds are renewed by reading His word, praying, and seeking to know Him more. God had a perfect plan for me. As I continued to be obedient and do

His will, I had no idea about the blessings God had prepared for me. There were many questions, and many mysteries. I didn't know how God would prove himself, but I simply believed He would and you know what? He did.

> *"Do not conform to the pattern of this world, but be transformed by the renewing of your mind. Then you will be able to test and approve what God's will is-his good, pleasing and perfect will."*
>
> Romans 12:2 (NIV)

Chapter 4

Receiving the Miracle: Our Body

"For we walk by faith, not by sight."

2 Corinthians 5:7–8

It was a beautiful day. My family and I were taking a walk. My stepdaughter and I were bringing up the rear strolling along when we heard the cry of a kitten. We stopped, looked around and noticed a tiny white kitten trapped in a bush wrapped in barb wire. I reached in and pulled her out. She couldn't have been more than four weeks old. I have always had a love for animals and felt it was my obligation to rescue them and nurse them back to health. In fact, I had done so several times. So when I yelled ahead to my husband to see what we had found, he yelled, "Put it back! Put it back!"

Of course, you know how the rest of the story goes. We now had a kitten in the family. My stepdaughter named her Gabby and so desperately wanted this kitten to be her very own. But for whatever reason this kitten claimed my husband and I as her sole providers. We tried many things to assist our stepdaughter and Gabby in bonding. For instance, we tried locking them up together in my stepdaughter's room at night, but Gabby would just cry. When we couldn't take it anymore, we opened the door and down the hall Gabby ran and jumped into our bed. Well, we fell in love with Gabby.

Several weeks later, Gabby became very ill. Our veterinarian diagnosed her with panleukopenia. Panleukopenia is a highly contagious viral disease of cats. It is a leading cause of death in felines. Kittens are the most severely affected because their cells are rapidly growing and dividing. The likelihood of recovery is very poor. Over 90% of felines infected will not survive. I stood there listening to these details roll off our veterinarian's tongue but focused on Gabby, who could barely hold her head up. She went on to tell me if Gabby could survive for five days, her chances for recovery greatly improve. By day three, Gabby had gotten much worse. She could not eat or drink. My husband was using a syringe to keep her hydrated. On day four, I took her to a holistic veterinarian. I was hoping to get a different diagnosis, treatment, or even just some hope of survival. The news was the same. In fact, this doctor told me Gabby would not make it through the night. She instructed me to keep warm towels in her crate and this would comfort her as she passed. I left her office in total defeat.

I cried all the way home over that kitty we had come to love. I had never seen an animal suffer like that in sickness nor one as tiny as Gabby who fought like she did to live. I had poured my gift of nurture into this kitty and it wasn't enough. I put her to bed and walked into the living room. I began to pray. "Lord, please give me some hope. I have done all I can do. Please heal this little kitty, but if you choose not to, please Lord, don't let her suffer anymore."

I wondered if the Lord cared about such things or was He too busy taking care of much greater things. In that moment, the Spirit prompted me to look up, where my eyes rested on a devotional on the fire shelf. I opened it up randomly and my eyes fell on the words "Because of the Lord's great love we are not consumed, for his compassions never fails. They are new every morning; great is your faithfulness." Lamentations 3:22,23 (NIV). His Word was the portion my soul needed. I wrote the scripture on a piece of paper and taped it to Gabby's crate and placed it by my bed. My husband and I prayed over Gabby and surrendered the results to the Lord.

The next morning, I awoke and it was silent. My thoughts immediately assumed Gabby was gone, but in a split second she cried out. I jumped up to see her sitting upright in her crate. Her eyes were bright! I called my husband over to see. I opened the crate and she ran straight to the kitchen, as if she was hungry. I prepared her food and she ate. We were in utter shock, but I knew the Lord healed her. I called the veterinarian, who was in disbelief. She could not make sense out of what I was telling her. I simply said it was a miracle of God; it was only God.

I tell you the full details of this story, because God used it to teach me so many things I needed to know and believe. Most importantly, He taught me to walk by faith, not by sight. 2 Corinthians 5:7

I put this scripture on the wall in our family room so we would daily be reminded. It was a life-changing moment for me spiritually. If I had only allowed myself to focus on the things I was seeing, there would be no hope; but by faith we believe and see the hand of God. I didn't know at the time, but I would desperately need to understand and believe this truth for what was ahead. He used a kitten to do it.

God had given us some time to rest and catch our breath, but it was time to get busy working towards the mission in which He had called us to in Myrtle Beach. Most of the founding has been done in Greenville, South Carolina and had transitioned to the beach. Now, it was time to do the groundwork. I needed to get in the community and share the mission. I needed volunteers, pastors, and churches to come alongside me and support this work. I spent time going door to door just sharing my testimony. I worked at home sending out emails, working on logos, and a website in between the hours of home schooling my stepson. My husband was working out his resignation notice, so he was still traveling and not home during the week. I leaned on the Lord for all things. I planned our first event to introduce the ministry in which God had named *Coastline Women's Center: Pregnancy and Family Support*. I had no idea if anyone would show up, but I was walking and preparing in faith they would. Surprisingly, over 60 people came. At this event I obtained my first set of volunteers whom I would later train. I also gained the support of some area churches.

Next, we needed somewhere to bring to life the ministry God had birthed in me. My speaking engagements had increased. God was keeping me busy. He was giving me many opportunities to speak to the hearts of people. I was obedient and walked through every open door He presented me. Of course, there were many obstacles and struggles, but I discovered there was always something to learn from them. I was amazed at what God was doing through me as I served Him from a tiny desk and chair in the corner of our rented townhome. I was ministering to hurting women and leading them through the post-abortion Bible study. One of the supporting pastors was loaning me some office space if a situation would arise and I needed to counsel. It was enough to meet the current need, but I knew we were getting to the point where we needed more.

During this timeline, God blessed my husband with a local job and we were finally able to be together as a family since the move. It had been a long, hard six months. We lost a substantial amount of income, but we knew God would provide our daily bread. We had nothing but His promises, and He had always proved to be faithful. I was so glad to have my husband home. I knew God was going to use him greatly in the ministry. My husband could not clearly see how yet, but I could. As much as I wanted to hurry him along, I knew it was a process and God would call him in His own personal way, so I patiently waited. There was so much God had me walk through alone during the founding of the ministry. He was doing a great work in me. I didn't fully understand it, but as I walked by faith and obeyed God, He was purifying me, because He was anointing me to fulfil His purpose.

I so wanted my heart to be right before the Lord. Daily with pen and paper did I seek His face. I wanted Him to be proud of me. One day, I received a phone call. It was from our former pastor and friend. He had become a great mentor in my life and supported my husband and me greatly in our call. As we talked about some new developments in the ministry, he paused and said, "Honey, you are a Matthew 5:8 and I am so proud of you." I knew Matthew 5:8 was a beatitude but I couldn't remember for sure which one, so after the call ended I hurried to my Bible. There it read "Blessed are the pure in heart for they shall see God." My eyes filled with tears, my heart filled with joy, but to also be told "I am proud of you," I knew it came straight from the Heavenly Father. My pastor was just the vessel delivering the message. I knew I was in the center of God's will and He was pleased. So, I pressed on.

We needed a building, a location to open the doors of the ministry. We certainly didn't have the money to purchase something or even lease something. At this stage of growth, all startup costs and most of all financials needed had been provided from my husband and me personally. With his change in job, all extra resources were gone, so we knew God would fully have to provide it. I prayed and I waited. At times I felt anxious, but I tried to keep my eyes and ears open to any movement and direction from God. A journal entry from this season read "Today I feel so much better, peaceful. God is telling me to just slow down and enjoy His presence. There is no rush. I am to enjoy His blessings. Yield to His creative work in me, neither resisting or trying to speed things up. It is His timing only. I will enjoy God's tempo and hold His hand with childlike faith and trust. The way before me will open up step by step."

There were weary days and good days. Yes, there are consequences to disobedience, but there are also consequences to obedience. One of the consequences to obedience is warfare. Expect it. Why would you not? When you are in the center of doing God's will, the enemy will attack because He knows the impact you will have and He knows the blessings you will receive once you have endured. Then the blessing came. God led me to a godly man who offered us some space for the ministry. We met and he gave me a tour. It fit the need perfectly. It was over 1700 square feet. He went on to tell me there was a committee I would need to speak before. I would need to share the vision and publicly ask for the space, and it would be voted upon. The best part was if it was approved the space would be granted to us…wait for it…for FREE! This was a big deal. So I prayed and journaled, "Father please display your splendor in my heart and align my heart with my mind so you may be glorified in action and in truth."

The day came. I was preparing to go and present for the building space. I prayed "Lord have your way. Help me to obey. Help me to be strong and courageous." Now what I am about to tell you is another one of those defining moments when I know the Lord moved on my behalf because of my obedience. I was introduced and I went forward. I shared the mission and vision of *Coastline Women's Center*. I shared a bit of my own personal testimony and my passion for the great work. I shared our current need for working space so we could propel this vision of the Lord forward. Then, I stepped down. As my feet descended the steps, I knew I had given my all and it was up to God now.

The director of missions who had invited me to speak went forward and said he would like to make a motion for this to be discussed among the committee and voted upon at the next quarterly meeting. I thought, next quarter! Lord, that is too long. I began to pray on that pew with tears in my eyes. "Lord, please set these pews on fire. Please move on someone's heart to do something now, Lord, tonight." No one knew my request to the Lord. It was between Him and I alone. It was a desperate cry to Him.

As soon as I finished that prayer, a strong, bold voice came from the back of the room. "We don't need to wait another quarter. We need to move on this now. I make a motion to give space to *Coastline Women's Center* immediately."

"But my God shall supply all your need

according to His riches in glory by Christ Jesus." Philippians 4:19

I began to cry. Next, came a second to that motion, and they all agreed by saying Aye. It was a great movement of God on our behalf. Even as I write it now, recalling, and reading my old journal entries, chills are running up and down my body. I got the chance to personally talk to the pastor who jumped up on our behalf that night. He said he wasn't planning to, but God moved in His heart and told him to do it. Obedience. Obedience changed everything. The pew was set on fire.

That same week I was given the keys and our renovation began. Everything the Lord showed me in a vision was coming to life. Renovation began in late May, and on June 27, 2013 we opened our doors to the community. God had done it! Much hard work had gotten us to this point, but it was only the beginning. The next year, I worked hard taking care of those in need who walked through our doors. I mostly worked alone with the help of a few committed volunteers. My heart was sold on sharing the gospel to everyone who walked through our doors, knowing everyone's greatest need is a Savior.

So many times as I counseled and looked across

the room at young women facing an unplanned pregnancy, I saw myself. I remembered what it was like to be fearful and confused. I understood the need for compassion and understanding but, also the greater need for truth. I was determined to provide that through the ministry. When I wasn't counseling, I worked on policies, procedures, and creating work forms. It was a great responsibility and I was depending only on Him. Things would arise, and I knew there were folks I could call for advise, but the Lord would never allow me to do so. The Holy Spirit would whisper, *"I am your teacher and I will teach and lead you in the way I want it done."* I believed the Lord led me this way and is still leading me this way so only He can be glorified.

Also during that first year was a lot of emotion. My mind always thought of my baby Abagail in Heaven. I was so thankful knowing she was in the gracious care of Jesus. I still desperately wanted a child. I wanted to feel the miracle of life in my womb and wondered still if I ever would. I worked hard, loving and serving others. No one knew the depth of my own struggle. When you have been diagnosed with infertility and your desire is nothing but to have a child, it feels like the end. An end to a dream, a family, happiness, and fulfilment. You fight for hope. You wonder silently and painfully if you will ever hear the word mommy directed to you. You wonder if you will ever be the proud mother walking forward to dedicate your new baby. Unless you have gone through it yourself, it is hard to fully understand.

It was a painful, long season in my life. The strength that spilled out of me to do the things I did was only the supernatural strength of God. There were numerous conversations between me and my husband, who felt totally helpless. He couldn't fix it. Neither one of us understood, and now we were looking back over nine years' time of asking God for the blessing of a child that had not come.

You get to a crossroad in this struggle where you have to choose to live or die in your pain. I chose to live. I had come to a place of peace and accepted if God didn't do this thing, I would be OK. I chose to focus instead on all the other blessings around me. It had been a year since we opened, and I was beginning to see the great harvest. Mothers I counseled who chose to parent verses abort walked through the doors, thanking me, and placing their babies in my arms. I held them with such joy, such pride. I realized sometimes the blessings God chooses to give you come in different packages. I had reached a place where it was well with my soul. I began to pray differently. I told the Lord I accepted His will for me and if it wasn't for me to become pregnant and carry a child, to please take the desire away from me. He never did.

The ministry was busy. We took a leap in faith and hired an assistant to help me. We were operating off of less than a shoestring budget. Immediately after hiring the assistant, God provided a stable increase in our monthly giving that was enough to cover her pay. I was wearing many hats and amazed as I reflected on my past: former jobs and responsibilities, education – all of it had been used to prepare me for this appointed time to lead this ministry. The skills and talent the Lord had blessed me with were all needed to get the job done. Of course, none of it would have amounted to a hill of beans if the heart was not willing and obedient.

When it comes to our bodies in reference to obedience, we have to recognize that our strengths, talents, and even our sexuality are given to us by God to be used for pleasure and fulfillment according to His rules and purposes, not ours. Everything in the past had prepared me for this ultimate Kingdom purpose that even today I don't fully see and know. It is only for God to know. All we knew was to keep walking by faith. Faith was the only sure, concrete thing we had in our life. We spent a lot of time in the book of Hebrews where it says "But without faith it is impossible to please Him; for he that cometh to God must believe that He is, and that He is a rewarder of them that diligently seek Him." Hebrews 11:6

There were days when I was totally exhausted. Just when I thought nothing else could be added to my plate, I got an invitation from Heartbeat International to teach a workshop at their yearly conference. Heartbeat International is an international Christian association of over 1800 crisis pregnancy centers, providing assistance in education, training, and support services like legal advice and networking with other centers. So it was a complete honor to be contacted by them to teach and lead a workshop. The topic was abortion recovery and how to implement services into operating centers and grow them. It was a topic I felt very comfortable with, but time was the issue. I didn't have time to prepare the educational material and plan this trip with everything else I had to do.

As I prayed over the decision, I knew the Lord wanted me to do it. He led me to Hebrews 10:36 that read, "For you have need of endurance, so that after you have done the will of God, you may receive the promise." It said *after* I had done the will of God. I had to keep pressing forward. There was a point of completion I believed God was trying to get me to in this particular season of my life. My heart pondered what the promise was. I only hoped for one thing. I was hoping God would grant me the desire of my heart. I was hoping He would reward my diligence. So I went and taught the workshop. I was obedient.

During the next couple of months, God kept returning me to that scripture. I was journaling about it constantly. I was so busy trying to lead the ministry, I had lost track of calendar time. With my husband's change in job, and loss of greater income, there was beginning to be a financial struggle. His income was the only one we had. We came to the conclusion we could not afford the townhome we were renting. We knew we needed to find other housing. Just the thought scared me. I knew what was available out there in the price range we could afford, and it was not very comforting. So we prayed, and gave it to the Lord. We continued to search and found nothing. It felt like that homeless situation all over again, but we knew God would send a lifeboat.

We had become very active in a life group from

our church and made some great godly friends. One night after one of our gatherings, a couple we had grown quite fond of asked to speak to us. They began to tell us they purchased a home on the river and they were moving. We rejoiced with them. They went on to tell us they had been praying about what to do with their current home, and they wanted to talk more about it with us at a later time. We agreed and the conversation left us curious.

A few days later, we received a call from the husband, who said they felt led by God to offer us their three-bedroom home to live in rent-free for the first year. What! Were we hearing things? I mean this does not happen in today's world. We knew it was only God, and this man willing to obey Him. Of course we accepted, and I was so excited we would have an additional bedroom. I wondered what I should do with it, maybe an office? God met our need once again. With Him nothing is wasted and there is a reason and purpose for all things, so no surprise He had a plan for the third bedroom.

It was April 10, 2014 and time to pack again. Everything seem to be happening so quickly. I had become an expert in moving. A close friend who served in the ministry with me offered to come over and help me pack some boxes. We laughed and talked while we worked. We talked about things women talk about. I began sharing with her I was feeling a little foggy headed. Mentally, I didn't feel as sharp as usual. I was wearing a shirt I got from participating in a 5k walk for the unborn. My friend laughed and said "Well Jeannie, the back of your shirt does say "Are You Pregnant? Maybe you should take a test." I laughed and blew it off.

After she left, I began calculating the days of my cycle and realized I was a little late. I drew the conclusion in my mind it was just the stress of the move. I had taken so many pregnancy tests in the last 10 years and was already justifying why this one would be negative, like all the rest. I drove away with a car full of boxes. Something came over me, and I quickly pulled into the parking lot of a drug store. I went in and purchased a pregnancy test. It felt as if someone else was driving, and it was not me.

When I arrived at our new home, I left everything in the car. I walked in with nothing but the pregnancy test in my hand. I was all alone. It was by God's choosing we were alone. It was a place I was familiar with. I wondered while I began testing if God had me alone so no one else could see my disappointment and heartache. Did He have me alone because only He could rescue me? I stood there waiting for the one lonely line that would indicate a negative test.

But friends, this time, this divinely appointed time, the result was two lines! The test was positive! I thought I was seeing things. My eyes were so blurry from the tears, but it was positive! It was positive! I fell to my knees in that empty new home in thanksgiving to the Lord. Words cannot describe. He had me alone because He wanted all of me. He wanted all the glory. He wanted to gift His daughter whom He was so proud of in a very intimate way. Nothing else would do. All the scriptures I had been clinging to from my journal began flooding my soul.

> *"...after ye have done the will of God, ye might receive the promise."*
>
> Hebrews 10:36
>
> *"...and, this shall come to pass if ye will diligently obey the voice of the Lord your God."*
>
> Zechariah 6:15
>
> *"Delight thyself also in the Lord, and He shall give thee the desires of thine heart."*
>
> Psalms 37:4
>
> *"He maketh the barren woman to keep house, and to be a joyful mother of children."*
>
> Psalms 113:9

"...ye shall ask what ye will, and it shall be done unto you."
John 15:7

"For your shame ye shall have double..."
Isaiah 61:7

The greatest shame in my life had come from my abortion. The above scriptures were just some of the many the Lord used to encourage my soul as I prayed faithfully for a child. I wasn't sure what the double was in the Isaiah scripture but I was eager to find out. The more the world tried to convince me it would never happen I pressed harder into the Word of God. I chose to stand on His promises. It was all I had and it was all I needed. The doctor gave his report but I waited and trusted in the Lords report. Even though I had reached a place of peace in my infertility, I never gave up hope. Then, one God chosen day, I received my miracle. I discovered what the extra bedroom was for.

Then Jesus said, "

"The things which are impossible with men are possible with God."
Luke 18:27

Chapter 5
The Gift: Our Finances

"Bring all the tithes into the storehouse, that there may be food in My house, and try Me now in this, says the Lord of hosts, If I will not open for you the windows of heaven and pour out for you such blessings that there will not be room enough to receive it."
Malachi 3:10 NKJV

As I pondered on the timing of my pregnancy, I realized the ministry had just reached its first stage of stability. I knew my pregnancy was a divine gift, a reward for my obedience. God was beginning to bless the ministry more financially. The obedience we were walking through was opening our lives to more holy possibilities. Every gift was a result of obedience. By obeying the Lord, it was putting us in a position of prominence before Him. Charles Stanley put it like this: "For some people, the key may be love, faith, or service. I want to tell you that the key to God's heart is obedience." I had read so many stories in the Bible of how God provided for His children in their time of need but now I was living it. There were already numerous stories of His providence. From a worldly view and at times even on paper it may have looked like we didn't have much, but from a heavenly perspective we were abundantly rich.

As I progressed in my pregnancy, I knew I needed to hire an additional staff person. This person might assume my position or take over my responsibilities, because surely God was going to allow me to stay home and just be a mama. This assumption would lead me to another lesson learned. God's ways are not our ways. Sacrifice and surrender would continue but oh the blessings that came from obedience. Finally, the day our miracle was revealed. Did God choose to give us a little girl or boy? Everyone around us declared it was a little girl- mostly because of my testimony.

The truth is God does not replace babies. Each one is uniquely made by Him with their own beautiful purpose. I learned this as I was going through the abortion recovery Bible study. This was a new thing God was doing. I was reminded of Isaiah 43:18-19, "Forget the former things; do not dwell on the past. See, I am doing a new thing!" NIV

With anticipation, we all gathered by the beautiful Kingston Lake awaiting to see what color balloons would rise from the box labeled "He or She?" Then the moment came. Up they went! The crowd rejoicing! Many were in shock. Blue was the clue. We were having a little boy! God gave us a son. In my journal I wrote, "A perfect gift sent from above, a baby boy to protect and love." Our hearts were filled with Heavenly joy. His name would be called Luke.

One day, in walked a woman who had a passion for pregnancy crisis. She was moving to the area and wanted to serve. She previously spent years serving in a similar ministry. I thought, God has led this woman right to our doors. We had several conversations and through prayer we believed she was to step in and assist in operations. So we took another leap of faith and hired her knowing God would provide the funds to pay her. As long as we were confident of hearing His voice and obeying we knew He would provide, and He did. The by-products of obedience are confidence, comfort, joy, and contentment. Now, we had two paid employees, an administrative assistant and a director of client services. I was tickled pink. This allowed me time to prepare for our little Luke. I worked quite a bit from home. This was my first real balancing act. I bounced back and forth from working hard for the ministry and preparing to bring Luke home.

On December 16, 2014, Luke Carter Smith, entered into the world. Finally, I was experiencing what I had only heard of, what I had only dreamed of. I soaked in the truth of this little baby belonging only to me. I thoroughly enjoyed my maternity leave. We were so blessed with the gifts and visits of all our family and friends. They were rejoicing over Luke as much as we were. Many of them had walked our infertility journey with us. Many of them prayed earnestly God would bless me with a child, so Luke was their little miracle too. After the initial excitement was over and the visits stopped, I nestled in trying to figure out how to be a mama. God was faithful. Then, struggle began to set in and we faced some hard decisions.

I am going to get very transparent with you which is not out of the ordinary for those who know me. However, to my surprise when it came to our personal finances, I discovered I was very fearful.

THE GIFT: OUR FINANCES

Prior to serving in full time ministry, our careers provided much financial security. We had more than enough. Even after I resigned, my husband's career still provided financial security. Matter of fact, his career provided so well for us no other income was needed.

However, when God began calling my husband more into the ministry it meant letting go of our worldly security and depending completely on Him for all of our resources. Prior to Luke being born, my husband sensed God's call on him more personally. He began weaning his work hours down so he could work in the ministry more. This meant even less income for our family, but God was showing him how much he was needed particularly as we were seeking to become a medical clinic. My husband's medical background as a registered nurse with 16 years' experience was a great asset to the ministry, but there were so many other important roles he played. I watched as my husband wrestled with this decision. It was a big deal giving up his career. A man's role is to provide for his family and if he feels like he can't failure creeps into his being. My husband was fearful and it meant letting go of everything he had worked towards in his career. At this point, we had no insurance, no savings, and a baby. To say the least, I was feeling quite insecure. Many advised Carter to not resign from his job because he needed to provide for his family. Everything that seemed financially nuts to us seemed to be the direction the Lord was leading us. His ways are not our ways.

During my maternity leave, there proved to be a need for me back in the office. As much as I would have liked to let go and just raise Luke the ministry was only three years old and needed much of my attention. My husband and I tried to offset our schedules to care for Luke. When situations arose and both of us were needed in the office we hired a babysitter. This caused even more of a financial strain. Personally, we were financially struggling but no one knew. I guess you could say I was battling pride in that area of my life. You see, neither one of us had ever taken a dime from the ministry. It wasn't about money for us. Our heart was sold out to God and the vision He called us to. We had invested everything and wanted it all to go towards the mission. I didn't want anyone to ever think we were doing what we did for money. Many would ask, "Do you and your husband take income? I always took great pride in answering "No." Did you catch the word? Pride.

THE GIFT: OUR FINANCES

One particular day driving into the office I found myself very emotional. I cried most of the drive over. I was trying to pray but the words would not come. I was scheduled to lead a client through a Bible study lesson. I walked in carrying my briefcase and walked straight to my office. I lowered the brief case to the floor and plopped in my chair. My eyes locked on the handle of my briefcase. There was literally one string holding the handle together. As I glared at the handle, tears filled my eyes. I begin to sob as I spoke out "Lord this ragged briefcase reminds me of myself. I am barely holding it together." At that moment a prayer warrior that faithfully came in and prayed for the ministry walked out of the prayer room and into my office. By this time snot was dripping down my lip. She asked me what was wrong. Typically, I would not have shared so quickly about something very personal but that day I didn't care. That day I was desperate to have God move on *my* behalf. Most days I shared the prayer requests of others but this day I had one of my own. I began to pour it out and tell her how we were financially struggling. How it was difficult to even put food on the table. No more pride.

She looked at me, took my hand, and said,

"Jeannie, do you not take a salary?" I answered, "No." She then went on to say, "This is not good. I have watched you put value and worth on everyone around you. Now, I am realizing you are not allowing God to be put value on you. You are not receiving what He wants to give you." One word, Pride. At that moment, I looked down in my lap. I was feeling so beat up. In my lap was the Bible study book I was getting ready to use with my client. The title of the study was "<u>A Jewel in His Crown</u>" by Priscilla Shirer. My tears were dropping on the subtitle of the study "<u>rediscovering your value as a woman of excellence</u>." Really God? I mean His message could not be more clear. My prayer warrior was right. God had sent her to deliver a message to me. She went on to ask me, if you were seeking to hire a CEO to take your place, would you offer them a salary? I agreed, I would. She then said, well God hired you. He wants to offer you a salary. Wow. I was speechless. She left and I went to see my client. I felt encouraged, uplifted, but God was not done yet.

About an hour or so later, I saw her walk back in. I was busy talking to a family in the lobby. She motioned me and waved a purple envelope in the air. Later that day, I retreated to my office and there on my desk was the purple envelope. As I opened

THE GIFT: OUR FINANCES

it, $1000.00 fell in my lap! I recorded her written words in my journal "Jeannie, I am sowing seed into your salary! Please read 1 Timothy 5:17-19. The worker deserves his wages. I love you. Get your foot up and finish the race!" One little purple envelope and one obedient prayer warrior changed my life forever. She said when she left that morning God spoke, told her to go home, get the squirrel money she was saving, and give it to me. She was obedient. A simple act of obedience changed my life. It was through her obedience I learned my value and how to receive in grace.

The time had come. My husband obeyed God and fully stepped out of his secular job. We were now dependent on God to provide for the ministry and our family. Our board of directors brought us both on salary. This decision strengthened the ministry and it began to flourish even more. With humility and boldness, we fiercely led the ministry into the next growth of our vision. We became a pregnancy medical clinic which enabled us to provide ultrasound to those mothers considering abortion. The day had come we could offer our very first scan. Our staff was so excited. Much training and hard work had brought us to this day. It was a young couple considering abortion. We were using an old machine but it was able to do the job. God gave us all a surprise. The scan revealed not one precious baby but two! Immediately the Holy Spirit reminded me of Isaiah 61:7 "For your shame ye shall have double...everlasting joy shall be unto them." The couple could not deny the double blessing God had given them and they decided to carry and parent.

Soon after we became medical, God provided a brand new ultrasound machine. A total of $29,000 was raised in nine weeks. Then God allowed the next growth of our vision and provided us a second location. This would allow us to reach more clients in a different part of the county. He also directed me step by step towards another part of the vision which I can't fully reveal yet, but its extraordinary and will display His splendor. This all happened before the year ended. This particular year, I have been in awe of God's providence. He has done so much already I can barely wrap my mind around it. Just recently, we were awarded $80,000 which was the result of complete obedience. Right behind it came another unexpected gift of $20,000. God also threw in a company truck! Gifts were coming from all directions. Big gifts, small gifts, but all with immeasurable value. For all the hard work, sacrifice, obedience, the Heavens declared reward and rained blessings all over us. So, at this point I think it's important to not miss the timeline we are talking about, because it is only God that could do a movement like this. Pay close attention to the details and the trail of blessing that came from every act of obedience. To Him be the Glory!

Let's review:

2009 - The gift of healing from my abortion.
    God called me to write my story.

2010 - Began writing my first book
    (Shattered *into Beautiful*)

2011 - My book was published and released.
    I received the call from God. Will you go?

2012 - The vision, the surrender, the move

2013 - The **opening** of the ministry.
    A budget of $28,000.

2014 - Hired Staff, Birth of Luke
    (my miracle after 10 years of infertility)
    A budget of $48,000

2015 - Began training to become a Medical clinic.
    Established our yearly Fundraising Gala.
    Budget $117,000.

2016 - We began operating as a
   Medical Clinic, Gift of second location.
   Budget $205,000.

2017- Began serving clients in second
   location, more vision birthed.
   Budget currently projected at $300,000.

To obey is better than sacrifice. This is summed up in 1 Samuel 15:22. Even during our personal financial struggles we never stopped giving back to God and advancing His kingdom. We gave our time, our talents, and our money. It's all His anyways. He simply loans it to us to serve Him and live an abundant life. We strive to be good stewards of everything the Lord provides. It has been a time of testing, a time of learning, a time of obedience. There is a spirit on your money. It is one of God or Satan. If the Spirit of God is on your money you will be generous. If the Spirit of Satan is on your money you will be selfish. There is a reason Matthew 6:21 reads "For where your treasure is, there will your heart be also." Prior to this scripture Jesus was explaining we should store our treasure in heaven rather than earth. When you begin walking out a life of obedience you can rest assure God will address your finances. We have to acknowledge all the resources we have ultimately come from God. Our job is to be managers of them not owners. He does not tempt, but He does test, and we are told those who are faithful with little will be faithful with much. Luke 16:10

There is a phrase of words that encouraged me greatly during this financial season. I journaled, "Give. Our poverty shall be turned to wealth, and we will be free of any anxieties concerning financial matters. Stay focused on God's economy not the one of this world. Giving to God immediately becomes spiritual currency. For our obedience, God will multiply our blessing." I also wrote these words on an index card and posted it to the wall above the desk we sat at weekly to review our finances. Another promise found in the Bible comes from Deuteronomy 15:10 which reads, "You shall surely give to Him, and your heart should not be grieved when you give to Him, because for this thing the Lord your God will bless you in all your works and in all to which you put your hand." NKJV I can tell you He has fulfilled His promise and we sit in wonder of how much is leftover week after week. Not only are we committed to giving personally, but also giving an offering from the ministry. Our mission statement at *Coastline Women's Center* is, "*To transform the lives of those we serve by sharing the Gospel of Jesus Christ, focusing on the whole being, upholding the sanctity of life, and dealing with the impact of pregnancy and abortion on individuals and their families.*" In addition to our mission, we pledge to support other ministries we believe have a great impact for the kingdom. We currently are giving locally, at state level, and internationally. The organizations we give to make it top priority to share the gospel and are reaching lost souls.

It has amazed me time and time again how God has provided. There just isn't enough space for me to write all the stories of how He has gifted my family and the ministry because of our obedience. There is not enough space to quote all my journal entries which reflect His voice, His direction, His guidance, His providence, and His rewards. Actually, I have found it difficult to narrow my journey with the Lord thus far in just a few chapters. It simply cannot be fully captured. As much as I love telling His stories, I have come to realize the greater part of the journey is meant only for Him and me, but I hope you have caught a glimpse.

THE GIFT: OUR FINANCES

When God called me and my family we made a commitment to stay loyal to Him, because He is loyal to us. We committed to keep our eyes on Him and glorify Him in everything we did. We committed to stand strong for Christ no matter what came our way. We have taken leaps of faith time and time again. The order and formula of how God leads and provides for us is not common to man and not by the standard of man. In fact, the world may say it cannot be done but God says it is done and finished! What is important is we do not get hung up on the formula, but stay focused on the source. The formula may change, but the source meaning Him, will never change. God likes to give His blessings in different ways, in new ways. He has a faithful track record which encourages us to not be fearful, but excited about each new step of faith. The journey just gets richer! We can trust Him. You can trust Him! I believe His unique formula was to prove to our audience how marvelous and great He is. Every blessing and gift has been by His hand. It is all because of Him! God did it all. We were just His servants, the vessels, in which the work could be done. What could God do through you? What is stirring in your heart right now? Embrace it, obey it!

"For the eyes of the Lord run to and fro throughout the whole earth, to show Himself strong on behalf of those whose heart is loyal to Him."

2 Chronicles 16:9 NKJV

Chapter 6

First Love: Our Future

"Nevertheless I have somewhat against thee, because thou hast left thy first love."

Revelation 2:4

When God places you in leadership there comes a time when you learn to seek His direction verses man. Don't get me wrong. Godly counsel is needed in our lives, but it should never suppress the defined, powerful voice of God. There will be times when your decisions go against what man suggested, but we are not accountable to man. We are accountable to God. He knows what is best. He knows the purpose and plan He has for you. You must walk in it. It may even be painful, but joy will come.

There is no greater love than a mother can have for her children. Through the gift of parenting, we come to understand the love our Heavenly Father has for us. When Luke was born, I assumed God would allow me to stay home with him, after all, I had waited so long for a child. That was not God's plan. The ministry needed me, but Luke needed me too. I was struggling. For the first 12 months, I was able to manage. I took Luke to work with me every day, but as Luke got more mobile it was very difficult to care for him at work. My husband and I tried to rotate our schedules to keep Luke at home, but it brought even more stress upon our lives. The time had come. A decision had to be made. I would need to get care for Luke, or step down from my ministry role, and stay home with him. We began to pray and research our options. We discovered quickly the only care for Luke we could afford was daycare. The thought of placing my son in the hands of strangers ripped my heart out. I refused, and continued taking Luke to work with me.

One particular day, I faced the hard reality our office was not a safe environment for Luke. I sat in my office and cried. Then the Holy Spirit whispered to me, *"I gave him to you, now I need you to give him back to Me."* I knew the Lord was asking me to let go. I was trying to control the situation, as if I knew what was best for Luke, rather than the one who created him. The Lord was leading us to place Luke in daycare for this season. We obeyed. During this time of decision making, many voices came my way. I was told, "you need to step down from the ministry and raise your son." I was told, "God didn't give you this miracle for you to put him in daycare." I was told, "You need to make sure you are putting God first, family second, and ministry third." I appreciated their concern. I did listen, but did they think this was a decision we didn't pour prayer over? God was very clear and we had to obey. I trusted God was going to make a way, in His timing, to allow me to be with my son.

I thought of Abraham, and the sacrifice God asked of him concerning Isaac. God just wanted Abrahams' faithfulness to be proven. This was my Abraham moment. When God personally calls you to a mission, it's not just considered ministry, and then falls in third priority. Instead, it reflects an intimate relationship with Him. One of obedience, or disobedience. One of love, or not love. Ministry is the result of the relationship, it's the by-product, it's the fruit, it's the service. God must remain our first love. God was Abrahams' first love. God was Moses' first love.

I could not wait to write this chapter because of what it means to me. My eyes well up in tears as I position myself to finish this letter to you. I hope you will grasp the depth of its importance. This chapter is on Love. Love and obedience are woven together. When you love you obey. I have told you many stories of my own as an example. I want to remind you the same God in the Old and New Testament is still in business today. He is still doing miraculous things on behalf of those who love and serve Him.

As we opened this book we were setting up camp, preparing to hear from God. let's return back there and jump back into the scene. Moses has received some words from God. He has spoken them to the people and they promised to obey, but they fell into mischief. They broke the very first commandment given by God found in Exodus 20:3 which read, "Thou shalt have no other gods before me." Even though they had seen the invisible God in action, they still wanted to elevate the gods they could see. They wanted to obey God when it was convenient and ignore Him when it was not. We are no different. Over and over God showed His mercy and love for them, but they trampled on it. God could not work within them when they chose to elevate themselves, or idols above Him. Moses pleaded for the people. In Exodus 34, God tells Moses to climb to the top of Mount Sinai. God gives him specific instructions and Moses obeys. God meets with Moses and reveals His character. In Exodus 34:6,7 it reads, "Yahweh! The Lord! The God of compassion and mercy! I am slow to anger and filled with unfailing love and faithfulness. I lavish unfailing love to a thousand generations. I forgive iniquity, rebellion, and sin. But I do not excuse the guilty. I lay the sins of the parents upon their children and grandchildren; the entire family is affected-even children in the third and fourth generations." NLT. Moses pleaded again that God would forgive their sin and rebellion.

I find it humbling, a Holy God, did not give Moses a vision of His power and majesty, but rather of His love. Over and over God tried to teach them how to obey and live as holy people. Over and over God provided for complaining people. Moses was faithful to pray for them but in Numbers 14:18 as he reminds us of the characteristics of God, he also reminds us by no means does God clear the guilty. God condemned the people to wander 40 years in the desert. God went on to say in Numbers 14: 21-22, "But as truly as I live, all the earth shall be filled with the glory of the Lord. Because all those men which have seen my glory, and my miracles, which I did in Egypt and in the wilderness, and have tempted me now these ten times, and have not hearkened to my voice; Surely they shall not see the land which I sware unto their fathers, neither shall any of them that provoked me see it:"

God's judgment came in the form the people feared the most. They were afraid of dying in the wilderness, so God punished them by making them wander in the wilderness until they died. We serve a good but just God. The people of Israel had a clearer view of God than any people before them. They had His laws and His presence. Their refusal to follow God after witnessing His miraculous deeds and listening to His words made the judgement more severe. How much greater is our responsibility to obey and serve God?

Through my study, God gave me compassion for the Israelites. In Exodus 6:9 it reads, "Moses spoke thus to the people of Israel, but they did not listen to Moses, because of their broken spirit and harsh slavery." ESV. The Israelites did not have the ability to believe the promises of God because of what they had gone through. I wonder what you may be going through right now. I wonder if your spirit is broken. Maybe you feel like there is no hope for you because of your lifestyle. Maybe you have endured so much pain you don't know how to believe, or not sure you believe in anything at all. Maybe just like the Israelites you don't have the ability to believe the promises of God. The Israelites had been in slavery. They had endured a lot. They did have a broken spirit, but God wanted to replace their broken spirit with freedom and purpose!

What does purpose look like for you? In what area of your life do you need freedom? Our culture has learned to live in slavery. It breaks my heart to see so many stuck in slavery and not able to progress to their Promised Land. The greatest weapon you have to live in freedom is your mind. Paul put it like this, "Do you know that if you present yourselves to anyone as obedient slaves, you are slaves of the one whom you obey, either of sin, which leads to death, or of obedience, which leads to righteousness? But thanks be to God, that you who were once slaves of sin have become obedient from the heart to the standard of teaching to which you were committed, and having been set free from sin, have become slaves of righteousness." Romans 6:16-18 ESV

Where the Spirit is, freedom is. In John 8:31 Jesus says, "…If you hold to my teaching, you are really my disciples. Then you will know the truth, and the truth will set you free." Again He speaks in verse 34, "Very truly I tell you, everyone who sins is a slave to sin. Now a slave has no permanent place in the family, but a son belongs to it forever. So if the son sets you free, you will be free indeed." NIV

Do you want to leave a legacy of freedom or captivity? Right now, this very moment, God wants to offer you a first class ticket to a brand new life! He wants to give you purpose and freedom! So how do you move forward into purpose and freedom that makes you eager to jump out of bed every morning? The answer was spoken by King Solomon who was considered to be the wisest and richest man that ever lived. After reflecting upon his entire life he said everything was meaningless except these words, "Now all has been heard; here is the conclusion of the matter: Fear God and keep His commandments, for this is the whole duty of man. For God will bring every deed into judgment, whether it is good or evil." Ecclesiastes 12:13-14 NIV

As you sit before the mount, what is God asking you to do? Is your life marked by obedience to God and His Word? Can He count on you to respond to His will? Some march courageously and obediently into God's plans and purposes while others wander meaninglessly. Let's consider Joshua.

The good news is Israel (the new generation) does enter into the Promised Land! God spoke to Moses and instructed him in Numbers 27:18 ... "Take thee Joshua the son of Nun, a man in whom is the Spirit, and lay thine hand upon him;" Moses obeyed and appointed Joshua as his successor. When Moses was nearing his last days, he commissioned Joshua and the change in leadership began. This commission happened in Deuteronomy chapter 31. I want to stop right here and tell you something. These stories of the Old Testament are very relevant today. Exactly one year before God spoke to me, and directed our move to Myrtle Beach, He took me to this same passage. I wrote the date 2.11.10 beside these words in my Bible. Recorded in Deuteronomy 31:11-13 it reads, "When all Israel is come to appear before the Lord thy God in the place which He shall choose, thou shalt read this law before all Israel in their hearing. Gather the people together, men, and women, and children, and thy stranger that is within thy gates, that they may hear, and that they may learn, and fear the Lord your God, and observe to do all the words of this law; And that their children, which have not known anything, may hear, and learn to fear the Lord your God, as long as ye live in the land whither ye go over Jordan to possess it."

God was already telling me what to do before He had even revealed the place He chose to send me. In the ministry in which we serve today, we obey these very commandments. We gather women, men, and children. We gather strangers at our gates. We offer them a cold drink of water and the gospel of salvation. We teach them and their children the Word of God.

Just before Moses died, he went up from the plains of Moab, and climbed Mount Nebo. Moses was not allowed to enter the Promised Land because of his disobedience to God, recorded in Numbers 20:11. Although he could not enter, God in His mercy showed him its beauty from the peak of Mount Nebo. In Deuteronomy 34:4 the Lord said to Moses, "This is the land I sware unto Abraham, unto Isaac, and unto Jacob, saying, I will give it unto thy seed: I have caused thee to see it with thine eyes, but thou shalt not go over thither." Scripture tells us next, Moses died in the land of Moab, and God himself buried him in a valley, in the land of Moab. No man still today knows of his burial place. Can you imagine the love God had for Moses? How honoring, God himself, would choose to bury His servant Moses.

FIRST LOVE: OUR FUTURE

It is no surprise to me in Jude 1:9 we are told, Michael the archangel had to fight the devil over Moses' body. When I read this story, I tear up, because I can sense in my spirit the love. God was his Father, but they were also friends. It was a love relationship reciprocated. Moses was 120 years old when he died. He is known as Israel's greatest prophet. When I think about what defines Moses as such a great leader, I think of his love for God and his obedience. Because of his obedience, Moses saw great signs and wonders. He spoke directly to God, and God spoke directly to him. God stood with him. Even though Moses didn't see God's face, He did see God. There was never another prophet chosen to experience God this way, but yet he still was disciplined, because of his disobedience. So, it is true, we receive blessings for obedience and punishment for disobedience. When we punish our children because of their disobedience, we don't do it because we want them to suffer. No, we do it out of love. So does our Heavenly Father.

After the death of Moses, God called Joshua. In Joshua chapter 1, God told him to arise, and take all the people into the land He had promised. God told him to be strong and courageous and he would prosper him. Joshua could not be fearful or discouraged. Fear would have caused him to believe he could not overcome, and have victory in what God called him to do. We are no different. Fear paralyzes us. Fear quenches the Spirt. It keeps us from reaching our greatest potential. God knew we would have fear which is why "Fear not" is the most repeated commandment in the entire Bible. If Joshua would have fell captive to these thoughts, God would have found someone else to do the job. But no, Joshua stayed strong. He knew he could not lose with God on his side. Joshua became known as a conqueror! Like Joshua, we have to choose this day whom we will serve. In Joshua 24:15, Joshua said, "…but as for me and my house, we will serve the Lord." Every day the Lord sets before us choices. We have to choose. Look at these two commands:

> *"Hear, O Israel: The Lord our God is one Lord: And thou shalt love the Lord thy God with all thine heart, and with all thou soul, and with all thy might. And these words, which I command thee this day, shall be in thine heart:"*
>
> Deuteronomy 6:4-6

"See, I set before you today life and prosperity, death and destruction. For I command you today to love the Lord your God, to walk in obedience to Him, and to keep His commands, decrees and laws; then you will live and increase, and the Lord your God will bless you in the land you are entering to possess. But if your heart turns away and you are not obedient, and if you are drawn away to bow down to other gods and worship them, I declare to you this day that you will certainly be destroyed. You will not live long in the land you are crossing the Jordan to enter and possess. This day I call the heavens and the earth as witnesses against you that I have set before you life and death, blessings and curses. Now choose life, so that you and your children may live and that you may love the Lord your God, listen to His voice, and hold fast to Him. For the Lord is your life, and He will give you many years in the land He swore to give to your fathers, Abraham, Isaac, and Jacob."

Deuteronomy 30:15-20 NIV

Obedience is a matter of the heart. If your heart is pressing into God, He will fast track anything. In Revelation 3:8 it reads, "I know thy works: behold, I have set before thee an open door, and no man can shut it: for thou hast a little strength, and hast kept my Word, and has not denied my name." Here Jesus is talking about the obedient church. If we are obedient to God, He will give us opportunities we never thought were possible. He will promote us, He will fight for us, He will uphold us. Some of my other favorites when marching in obedience are:

> "...Do all that is in thine heart: turn thee; behold, I am with thee according to thy heart."
>
> 1 Samuel 14:7

> "Fear thou not; for I am with thee: be not dismayed; for I am thy God: I will strengthen thee; yea, I will help thee; yea, I will uphold thee with the right hand of my righteousness."
>
> Isaiah 41:10

> "Call unto me, and I will answer thee, and show thee great and mighty things, which thou knowest not."
>
> Jeremiah 33:3

I am a story teller. I love to tell stories, God's stories. True stories are always more interesting. Don't you like to watch a movie based on a true story rather than one of fiction involving imaginary events and people? I believe God has made himself very real and alive to you through this book. You have read true stories, past and present. Yes, stories of the Bible, but also my own stories. If Moses could sit down with you right now, he would ask you to follow after the Lord God Almighty. He would ask you to obey Him and love Him above all other persons. I want to ask you the same. Obedience is a gift. Obedience is a chance for us to experience an all-powerful God! Obedience unleashes power in your life. Through obedience, God answers prayer. The enemy will try and choke out your walk and growth with God. He will cause distractions and create hindrances to keep you from reaching your full potential with God. But don't let him. As we reflect upon just a few examples, consider what others will say about you. How will your story end?

Through obedience- Noah built the ark

Through obedience- Abraham became the founder of the Jewish nation.

Through obedience- Moses led God's people out of Egypt.

Through obedience- Joshua led the Israelites into their God-given homeland.

Through obedience- Paul established the Church of Jesus Christ with both Jew and Gentile.

Through obedience- John provided the identity of Jesus Christ and the revelation to the church.

Through obedience- Jesus became the lamb of God. Taking on the sins of the world so no man would perish, but have everlasting life in the presence of Almighty God.

Through obedience _____ ...
\qquad\qquad\qquad Your name

I have learned so much about obedience. You know, I think it's God's way for changing people. I have certainly been changed. I am certain Moses and Joshua were changed. I have to come to realize, our assignments on this earth is our only opportunity to sacrifice, and to give an offering to our Lord. Only on earth, do we have the opportunity to give thanksgiving through difficulties and sorrow. On earth, is there only the opportunity to choose Him as Savior, and to overcome the world by the Holy Spirit within us. We must seize these precious times now. We must be obedient now!

We will never get these opportunities again for in Heaven there will be no need. In Heaven, the trials, opportunities, and tests will all be over. In Heaven, there will be only endless days of Joy and Praise! What a day it will be when my Jesus I shall see! Until that day comes, I am asking you to not forget God. Oh how I love Him. I love Him. There is no greater friend I have. If you love Him, He will make himself known to you in such an intimate way, just as He did Moses. He has not changed, and He desires your love. It is the greatest love affair. It is a love you can't fully comprehend. It is a love so underserving, but He loves you anyways, and He just wants you to love Him back. Our obedience to Him is love. It is His love language. I want you to know as I write this very paragraph tears are streaming down my face because of Love, His love. I want to encourage you today to return to your first love, Jesus. Let me introduce you. He is:

King of Kings.

Lord of Lords.

Redeemer of all men.

Light of the World.

Most High God.

All sufficient One.

Master.

Lord of Peace.

Eternal God.

Savior.

The Great I Am.

And this is just a few of His mighty names. I know it is easy to get distracted. It is easy to put Jesus on the back burner. Life sometimes comes at you and takes over. You don't mean to disregard Him. It just happens. It happened to me. I was busy, busy *serving* the Lord. The demands of the ministry filled my days, my hours, my minutes. There was nothing left for Him. Then one day, I finally got still enough to hear Him say, *"You have forgotten me. You have forgotten your first love. I don't want your service first. I want you, then your service."* Then God led me to Revelation chapter 2, which defines the loveless church. I was heartbroken. I dated it within my Bible. It was 2015, two years after our ministry opened. God so clearly spoke to me, verse 2, "I know thy works, and thy labour, and thy patience…" verse 3, "…for my name's sake hast thou labored, and not fainted." Verse 4, "Nevertheless I have somewhat against thee, because thou hast left thy first love." It was a turning point for me. I am not the only one this has happened to. I am certain it happens to other ministry leaders quite often as well. We cannot forget our love relationship with God is where it all begins. John MacArthur put it this way, "Far from being a drudgery, Christian obedience is thus the bond of our relationship with Christ and the source of our deepest joy." It is the most important relationship in our lives. Don't neglect it. Do not forget God. Remember all the ways He cares for you, provides for you, protects you, loves you.

My Pastor, Dr. Hampton Drum, took us through a sermon series as I was writing this book. It was called the "*Strength of Obedience.*" Perfect timing right? Dr. Drum said, "The challenge of a lifetime is to obey the Lord." He also said, "Tragically, too few see the enormous value of obedience and therefore never pay the price to obtain its rewards!" I couldn't agree more. Can I just tell you, God has already prepared something He wants to give you. Can I tell you, He is "… able to do immeasurably more than all we ask or imagine, according to His power that is at work within us." Ephesians 3:20 NIV. The secret is obedience. Charles Stanley put it this way, "I know from experience that obedience has to be a priority in every believer's life. It is the only way you will ever become the person God wants you to be and the only way you will ever achieve the things in life that He has so wonderfully prepared for you." So how do we obey God with our future? By deciding to make service to God and man the main purpose of our life's work. We are all called. Called to be saved. Called to share the gospel of salvation. Called to teach and make disciples.

It was late in the afternoon when we received a call from a former client. I was told by a coworker, "Jeannie you need to take this call." I greeted the caller, and her voice cracked as she spoke the words, "I know you probably don't remember me.

It has been almost two years. I came to your center seeking an abortion. I gave you all the reasons why I could not keep my baby. You were so loving and willing to listen. When I left, I kept hearing your voice say to me "God will provide." I want you to know, I kept my baby. I have a beautiful little boy and I can't imagine my life without him. I since moved to another state. I am now volunteering at a pregnancy center similar to *Coastline Women's Center*. I work as a counselor helping girls who are struggling with the same decisions, like I once was. You not only saved the life of my baby, you saved my life. I just wanted to say thank you." What a ripple effect! Friends, everything we do for the Lord matters. Every act of obedience matters. He places you divinely where you are supposed to be. So, go where you are sent. Stay where you are until God moves you. Give all you got until He calls you higher, ultimately, until He calls you home.

Our time together has come to an end. I want you to know I have endured great warfare as I have worked on this assignment from the Lord. I have overcome. I have also been given some exciting opportunities in leadership. As I prayed about these opportunities I wrestled with fear, but my faith proved to be greater. I knew with every step of faith taken, fear would fade, and confidence would take a front row seat. As a result, I have finally been granted the time with my son I desired. I was obedient. I want to ask you to do the same. It is time to leave the camp. Take a standing position, look out across the horizon, can you see your Promised Land? Be strong and courageous and march boldly into your future! This may be my last book, or it may not. If it is my last, I would like to leave you with some words spoken by a man named Reader Harris, "Probably some of the lasting of all preaching is with the pen." What is God asking you to do right now that will change your destiny? I know you can feel it rising up in you. You are ready... Go!

"If you love me, keep my commandments."
John 14:15

If you Love Me Obey Me

Bibliography

Dundas, Pat and Jim. (1994). Focus on the Heart: Hope National.

ESV. (1971, revisions in 2001, 2011, 2016). English Standard Version. Crossway Bibles.

McCasland, David. (1993). Oswald Chambers: Abandoned to God. Pg. 244

Meyer, Joyce. (1995). Battlefield of the Mind. Pg. 96.

NIV. (1984, 2011). New International Version. Zondervan (US).

NKJV. (1979, 1980, 1982). New King James Version. By Thomas Nelson, Inc. Publishers.

NLT. (2008). New Living Translation. Tyndale House Publishers.

Sorge, Bob. (2001). Secrets of the Secret Place. pg. 11,

Taylor, Howard. (1989, 2009 edition). Hudson Taylor's Spiritual Secret. pg. 20, 23

The Strength of Obedience. (2017). pgs. 5, 6, 11, 19

Washington, Martha. (2015). Reprint. The Heavenly Spheres: Character of Residents in Each, and Their Occupations.

If you Love Me Obey Me

Readers can contact the author at:
jeanniescottsmith.com

www.ingramcontent.com/pod-product-compliance
Lightning Source LLC
Chambersburg PA
CBHW021154080526
44588CB00008B/324